Richard A. Reid

The Man, The Music, and His Ministry

The Journey of a Living Legend

"Richard A. Reid: The Man, The Music, and His Ministry," by Laura A. Franklin. ISBN 978-1-63868-095-6 (softcover).

©2022 Laura A. Franklin. All rights reserved. No part of this publication may be reproduced, stored in a retrieval system, or transmitted in any form or by any means, electronic, mechanical, recording or otherwise, without the prior written permission of Laura A. Franklin.

Table of Contents

FOREWORD 1
PART 1, THE MAN (Sonata; The First Movement) 5
PART II, THE MUSIC (Minuet) 16
    Tributes & The Family Portrait 16
Tributes 18
    Damion Reid 18
    Darius Reid 24
    Henry (Shack) and Tayja Mashack - Family 29
    Billy and Mimi Thompson – Family 36
    Beatrice "Bea" Johnson, Musician - Family Friend 40
    Dr. Anthony L. Dockery – Richard & Althea's Pastor 43
    Jeannie Cheatham, World Class Piano Player/Musician/Singer/Songwriter 45
    A Family Friend 45
    Kevin Eubanks, World Class Acoustic Guitar Player 48
    Close Friend of the Family 48
    Nolan Shaheed, World Class Trumpet Player – Family Friend 54
    George Bohanon, World Class Slide Trombone Player, Family Friend 56
    John B. Nickens, III, Musician - Family Friend 58
    Carl Neder – Local Business Owner - Friend 62
    Debra Pettus - Family Friend 64
    Cheryl Brown - Family Friend 66
    Ryan Suchanek (Suh-hahn-neck) – A Friend from the Local Dodge Dealer 70

Richard A Reid: The Man, The Music, and His Ministry

Family Photo Album 74
Musical Tributes Continued with Dedications 87
Honorable Mentions 93
PART III, HIS MINISTRY (Allegro) 96
Part III, His Ministry, Cont., (The Family Circle) 102
THE FOURTH MOVEMENT (ROLLICKING) 108
Acknowledgments 113

FOREWORD
By Laura A. Franklin

DUKE ELLINGTON ONCE SAID, "The wise musicians are those who play what they can master."

The day of my first interview with the family, I arrive in the early afternoon on a warm, summer day in the 16th month after the Covid-19 pandemic has begun. I am one of the few who enters through the front door. I knock heavily as I've always done; this is how the family members know it's me. I am greeted by the eldest son, Damion. Though he is wearing a mask, I can tell he has a bright smile on his face. The Queen of the house, Althea, stands behind him almost as if she is hiding. She, too, greets me with a masked-covered bright smile and says, "Good morning." I have known the Reid Family more than four decades and have been close with them now for over 25 years. My mother and Althea were prayer partners, but most importantly, dear friends. Their relationship was tied together by strings of laughter, tears, prayers, wonder, and delight as they would discuss numerous topics in "The Shed." The Shed is a place where not many are invited, and it's a place for *reserved* conversations.

During the initial interviews, Richard is surrounded by his wife Althea, and their sons Damion and Darius. It is evident that he is loved and respected by his wife and children by the way they interact with one another in silence, and in speech. Together, The Reid Family is a presence that fills an entire room as well as much of the outdoor space. They present a strong, united force that is not to be taken lightly. They are a quadruple threat; a modern day

Fantastic Four with intellectual education, musical talent, tenacity, and wisdom. Individually, they offer the same strength, and are pieces of one another that break off just enough to plant their own seeds that have grown into a garden of interwoven, strong, and healthy branches that consistently reconnect without disruption to the others' growth, leaving room for individual plantings yet to take root. They are a humble lot that stand on the strong foundation of their faith, and their love for family that has assurance from the promises of the Word of God.

Richard is revered and respected by all who truly know him. He is a man who was given opportunities that have allowed him to follow the plan God laid out. He is a man that loves his family, and by many other accounts from those I have interviewed, he has an affection and an adoration of his boys that is only known between a father and his sons. They were rambunctious as kids, and the conversations they had on car rides, in their rooms, and especially in the shed were not only preparation, but an investment for which he has received a full and extensive return.

Richard beams with pride each time he speaks of them, but when others speak about his sons his elevated shoulders and inflated chest at the mention of their names speaks more than he ever could. As our former Pastor, Dr. McCall would say, *"he isn't bragging, he is just testifying."*

Yes, he is a living legend in the jazz, R&B, and gospel music industry, but in his own right, Richard Albert Reid is a living legend in his home. He is a man that has created a legacy of love for his wife of 44-plus years, a love of his boys, a love of his Faith, and a love of his music. For every gig he played, his first ministry was always to Althea, Damion, and Darius. For every note of every song played and written, and for every rehearsal, it was all to show those of us who trail behind him that nothing is more important than family. Life, to Richard, is one big gig. You show up, you show up on time, know your music, play with your heart, and leave them knowing you did your best and made them proud. That, my friend, is how you become a living legend with a legacy. I was afforded time alone with each member of the Reid Family while putting this project together. Each has their own unique personality on how they approached me. I have found them all both riddling and intriguing. Their *brand* proves they are one, and they are strong!

Here is a little back story to my relationship with Richard. When I was a child, I was afraid of Richard Reid. He looked as if he stood seven feet tall and his facial expressions made me believe he did not like children. I suspected he had a soft side because he had children of his own. Only, it went unnoticed until the year 2005 when I was an adult, and I was preparing to graduate from junior college. I mailed the Reid Family an invitation in celebration of me being the first in my family to earn a college degree. It was after one of the church services when I was having a conversation with Althea when he approached me. Our conversation went something like this:

"Hey! You graduatin'?" Richard asked with a grunt.

"Yes!" I replied to him with a smile on my face while trembling inside.

"Oh. Okay. Good. Keep it up!" He said.

Richard takes a step back to turn away but comes back to speak again.

"You know you sound just like your mother when you sing?"

"That's what I've been told so yea. I do." I replied trying to sound grown up.

"Yea. Okay." He answered. I knew he was putting me in check without putting me in check.

On this day, I learned he was not so frightening after all, and he cared enough to pay attention to me, and he supported my accomplishments. It is not often one gets to grow up around a man such as Richard Reid, a husband, a father, a world class musician in Jazz, R&B, and Gospel, a friend, and now, a living legend in those genres. It has been an absolute pleasure to know him thus far and getting to know him more through the shared stories from family and friends. Richard Reid, lovingly known to me as "Mr. Richard," has been there for me in silence and in clamor. I have witnessed the smiles, heard the laughter, and felt the emotions of anger, and tears of joy and pain as he reflects on his journey that includes illness, poverty, struggles due to segregation, hardships, his *"boy-to-man"* transformation, and his elevation musically, relationally, spiritually, and in his community. Richard Reid is just a great, all-around musician. He's also great at talking me into getting him treats that he is not supposed to have; treats such as jellybeans and chocolate candy bars. Again, this is the part that makes him human, a softie, and not so frightening.

To capture the purity and integrity of the relationships, each interviewee was allowed to tell his or her story without interruption. You will also notice that some timelines overlap. It is the Reid Family's hope that while you read through his memoir that you are encouraged, enlightened just a bit, and enjoy his journey. A reader may think this memoir is more about Richard's family than it is about him. However, to be a Living Legend, one must do legendary things such as raise two well-rounded, educated, God-fearing sons who have been poured into, stay faithful in his marriage to his wife at home and abroad, and keep God in the midst of it all while he plays on stage, and rests at home. All this manifests itself in ways we cannot imagine.

PART 1, THE MAN
Sonata; The First Movement

"A composition for one or two instruments, typically in three or four movements in contrasted forms and keys."

RICHARD ALBERT REID was born November 15, 1939, in Boston, Massachusetts to the late Mildred Iona (Morrison) Reid and John Conrad Reid. He is the youngest of seven children; three of whom passed away prior to Richard's entrance into the world. Many thought he would not live past infancy due to catching whooping cough, and other childhood diseases being prevalent during this era. He was sickly as a toddler, and modern medicines were not available then as they are now. When he was ill with whooping cough, his mother gave him homemade remedies to build up his immune system. Remedies like mustard plaster when he would catch a cold. The Mustard plaster with fried onions on brown paper would be placed on his chest with a little Vaseline, and it would pull the cold out of his chest. This, along with other home remedies was used to aid him with healing quickly. Richard mentioned that "they" didn't think he was going to live, but he says he fooled them. He never really asked questions about how his older siblings died, but suspects they, too, died from whooping cough. He accepted life as it was.

Richard shares a tender memory that was tucked away for many years that has decided to rear its head while he tells of his own health scare as a child. He remembers delicately when his oldest son, Damion, came down with a horrible cold as a child.

Richard called his mother, and he was told to do the same as she'd done for him when he was a child, and it worked. Richard laughs as he looks over at Damion remembering the fear they shared, and how Damion looks presently. His mother moved to Cambridge, Massachusetts to a house on Putnam Avenue; lovingly called Western Ave, the Black section. She then moved to "The Port", a predominantly white area which is where he grew up on Tremont Street; 39 Tremont Street. A lot of fights broke out between the blacks and whites; kids and adults alike engaged in the fist-of-cuffs. His mother got along with a lot of people on the street because she used to make soap out of bacon fat. People would save cans of bacon fat and bring it to her. It was considered one of the best soaps they'd ever had. She was open to sharing with the entire neighborhood and all were welcome. Many would stop by and be fed cake and sweet breads, and such. Those in the neighborhood all loved her as well.

There was one house that was considered a "three-family-house." Meaning, it had three families living in it. The walls were so thin, the cold came right through them, and it was the only house that had blacks living in it through the entire neighborhood. Richard feels it was because his mother was open to all of those in the neighborhood, and his mother used to clean white people's houses as well. When Richard was old enough to drive, his mother bought a 55 Ford, brand new. Many questioned how she was able to afford such a vehicle. *"She worked her butt off, ya know?"* Richard chuckles. Richard's father did janitorial work. When Richard was a child, his father was *"put away."* As he tells this part of history, it is clear by his body language that the pain still lingers. Richard explained that one day as his father was coming home from work, the police stopped and questioned him about being in that neighborhood. The officers didn't think he belonged there, let alone lived in Cambridge. His father got into a fight with the police, and they arrested him. For the better part of his childhood, his father was away. He was told that his father was placed in a mental institution because they couldn't put him in jail. His father pulled a knife on the cops so that was law enforcements justification for putting him in a mental institution. *"They figured he had to be crazy to be fighting cops."* Richard says. Richard was

Part I: The Man

not allowed to visit his father until he was a teenager. His mother visited as often as she could in Worcester, MA. When Richard was old enough, his mother would take him to see his father. His brothers Cecil and Bobby were now his father figures. At least fourteen years separate Cecil and Richard, and so the responsibility of making him a man fell on Cecil as the oldest. When he visited his father as a teen, his father asked him to see if he could get him out. It was not until Richard went into the Marine Corps and finished his assigned contract that he was able to get his father out of that institution.

As Richard reflects, he remembers his primary years being full of fights or playing in the park. The park (pronounced pahk, as spoken in his Bostonian accent) was at the end of the street on Western Avenue where the neighborhood kids would gather and play. Football was played in the streets and Richard was good at sports *when* he played. He didn't play in high school, only in primary school on playgrounds with broken glass, or dirt fields. Richard mentions that his family was the only black family in the area, and often, he had to walk home alone and pass by The Walsh's house, an Irish Family. Their kids would throw stones at him on his way home. Finally, one day, Richard met one of the boys, Joe Walsh, in the park (pahk), alone, and he was beat to a pulp. It was then that they stopped bothering him. There were gangs for each neighborhood. His neighborhood fought against the East Cambridge neighborhood, and various areas, and he was the one picked out, the only black that fought. The cops were always at his house informing his mother that Richard was in another fight. His mother always defended him. *"They're always picking on him because of his ethnicity."* She would say. This was a time of great segregation, and nothing has changed, in his words. *"All these years, at 81 years old, nothing has changed. Whitey thinks they're in charge. We are still the slaves as far as they're concerned."* He reflects. This is what he sees because he grew up in it.

Richard remembers, proudly, that no one messed with Cecil. Period. This is because Cecil was known to "kick a lot of tail." The older boys only picked on Richard when he was alone. When Richard was playing with other kids near the Cambridge Public

Works Department, people would park (pahk) their cars on the side street and go to work. A white guy parked his car in front, on the street. The kids that he was playing with, one of the white boys, broke the license holder on one of the cars. Richard was blamed for it because he was the only black boy outside playing with the kids. He was pointed out by the white boys to the owner of the vehicle. The white man slapped Richard across the face. Richard went home and his mother saw the fingerprints on his face. Richard told his mother what happened. *"It was Philios, Ma."* Richard said. Richard's mother told Cecil since he was the oldest child, and he was the one to talk to since his father was away. *"Tomorrow, I want you to point out to me the man that slapped you."* Cecil told Richard. Richard was not around to tell Cecil. He was out riding his bike. When the white man came to get his car, he brought his son with him because he knew there would be repercussions for what he did. The kids that Richard played with pointed out the correct man to Cecil. Cecil, then, proceeded to wipe the street with him. From that day forward, Cecil, nor Richard had any problems. Lovingly, Richard reflects, *"Cecil fought semi-pro. One Christmas, he bought me the best gift, a pair of boxing gloves. Cecil said he was going to train me to be a boxer, but that's not what I wanted to do. Cecil was a wicked fighter!"* He said with pride. *"I would call people off the street and get them to fight his brother. No one ever denied Cecil for two reasons; because they feared him, and they wouldn't miss the chance to beat up on a black boy."* Richard said. *"Cecil would threaten me to beat these white boys up, or else. And I did."*

Richard's mother was a Pentecostal church lady. No matter what you did during the week, church on Sunday was non-negotiable. While growing up, he had a good friend named Spanky Jones. Spanky's parents would tell him, *"Make sure you run with Reid because his family goes to church."* His mother was from Barbados, and she was in charge of cleaning the church, and she cooked for people at the church, and in the neighborhood. Richard shares that his family was not rich, and whatever money his mother made, she would make it stretch. His mother also cleaned rich, white people's homes to make money. Things that they didn't want anymore, cast-offs, they would give to her, and she would take it

Part I: The Man

and either give it to someone in need or keep it for herself. He remembers a time when a white family gave away a refrigerator. Then, it was called an Icebox then. A large block of ice was purchased and kept in the "freezer" part, and it would keep the entire icebox cold. When they no longer wanted theirs, Richard and his brothers would go pick it up and keep it. This is how they got their refrigerator. This was used until he and his siblings made enough money to buy his mother a new one.

Cecil and Bobby worked while Cynthia went off to college at Howard University. Bobby was not supposed to work because he was underage. He worked in Lord's Candy Factory. While cutting caramels, someone called Bobby's name. He turned his attention to that person, and while his head was turned, Bobby's fingers were cut off. Bobby was taken to the hospital where they grafted skin and tissues from his stomach, and then put his fingers back on. His mother was informed that she could have sued the company for a lot of money, but since there weren't any black lawyers they had a connection with, and it would not have benefitted her to sue, she didn't pursue it.

Richard was a solid "B" student in school. Though his mother preferred his marks be in the high 90's or 100's, she accepted the grades he brought home. His big sister Cynthia made sure he kept his grades up. His best subject in school was music. Richard's mother taught herself to play at home, and then she taught Richard and his siblings to play as well. Richard was in the school band, and he played the drums. Though the band leader made him play the drums, Richard gravitated to the Bass because of his mother. In school, Bobby wanted to play the saxophone, but the family could not afford to purchase the instrument. Cecil played "Boogey Woogey" on the piano, and Richard expounded on it. Richard would play the bass line on the guitar when his friends would come over. His mother did not allow them to play Boogey Woogey in the house, only gospel music because she was purely Pentecostal. Richard loved the bass because it was the foundation of the band. This speaks volumes to the kind of musician he is today. Many of his fellow band members speak of Reid as the standard; the foundation of it all. Instead of going to college, Bobby went to the Marine Corps after high school. Cecil stayed back as the male leader of the family and took on all the roles of a father to Richard. Randomly, Richard mentions his parents met in Barbados. His father entered America through Canada while working on a merchant ship. He isn't sure if they were married in the states or in Barbados, but he knows they migrated together. He, then, goes back to telling the remainder of the first part of his story.

According to *Cynthia's* plan, Richard was supposed to go to Howard University. Cynthia made sure he had all the necessary paperwork completed and campus connections as he prepared to graduate from high school, but Richard decided to join the Marine Corps instead because he wanted control of his own life. He went to Ringe Tech High School where he was taught a trade in auto mechanics, working as a typing clerk for a newspaper, and as an electrician. *"When you left, you went directly to a job."* Richard said. After acquiring those skills, he went to school at the Conservatory. Though his mother had no formal musical training, she helped Richard with his homework at the Conservatory.

As we embark into a new conversation on segregation, each of us shift our body in our chairs as if we are bracing ourselves for what's to come.

While in the Marines, Richard experienced a lot of racism. *"Many in the white population tried to pretend it wasn't there, but it was."* Richard says. He thinks back to a time when it affected his enlistment. *"For us to think racism was non-existent would be a fallacy."* He says with conviction. *"As long as you did as you were told and showed you could handle what they gave you to do, you were fine. Everyone was supposed to be treated equally, but the whites received preferential treatment. Marines didn't think black men could handle the training, but we proved them wrong."* Richard states. All of them had the same trainer. Each had to be on top of their game at all times. Richard reflects on a time when he had to wear working gloves during a punishment. *"These gloves were used for carrying dirty items, picking up trash, and pulling heavy equipment. I could not take off the gloves and had to wear them while trying to use the latrine. A spy or buddy was sent with me to make sure I did not take them off. I removed the gloves anyway. The drill sergeant asked the buddy if my gloves were*

Part I: The Man

removed, and the guy answered yes. Because the guy snitched, I was given extra duty, extra push-ups, and cross-squat jumps. Let's just say, the snitch got stitched afterwards." Richard said with a chuckle.

His first duty station was in Hawaii. He was in Chuck's Trucks. His brother Bobby was stationed in Hawaii as well. If Richard didn't pass the driving test, he would be sent to the infantry. Bobby, Richard's brother, helped him study at the end of each day. He took him through all the mechanics to make sure he wouldn't end up in the grunts (infantry). When it was time to take the test, he passed. Here's an example of what Richard's test included: Richard describes what the test entailed; *"There are five tumblers in a box. While driving, you are asked to brake and stop at a stoplight. When you stop, no tumblers are supposed to fall. The tumblers represent troops in the back of the truck, ammo, or other valuable items. The driver must know how to maneuver it through different types of terrain."* I am told that in Hawaii, they called black men, Brudda because Hawaiians related to us (blacks) more so than they did the white man. White men were called Holly's. Richard served four years in the Marines. He did not re-enlist because he didn't like the attitudes of the military personnel and there was too much racism.

After leaving the Marine Corps, Richard had various jobs. He often worked around cars (cahs) in Boston, a car wash and a used car mechanic for Waltham Automobile. He went to school to become a machinist and became a Shop Foreman. While being a foreman, he was playing with a music teacher in Boston. He would do gigs around town. He told his teacher he wanted to pursue music, and the teacher set him up to receive a scholarship to New England Conservatory. Richard reflects on this moment and says with a Cheshire grin:

"Once there, I met my wife, Althea. Meeting Althea was interesting. Althea was the top singer in the school, and he was the top bass player. She caught my eye by wearing short skirts all the time. As I walked into the cafeteria, she dropped her drink when she saw me. I was a pretty big dude so..." Richard says. Althea seems to have forgotten this part as she tries to interject. *"I was*

known not to take no mess from anyone. He and Althea had a class together; Music History." Richard says.

"When the class was over, I went to the front of the class to speak with the professor, and Richard walks up to me and says, *"You must be from Georgia because we don't have peaches like that in Massachusetts."* Althea remembers warmly. Althea's response was to stare at him because she felt what he said was lame.

"That was my first and last line. I didn't need another one." Richard says. *"Dating Althea was done properly."* Both their parents were in Michigan, and they were in Massachusetts going to school. Althea's mother, lovingly called "Boom Boom" drilled Richard when she finally met him to be sure he had the right intentions towards her daughter. Richard and Althea dated five years before they were married. Their age difference of 12 years was never an issue between them. When they went out on a date, Richard paid for all the meals. Some of their dates included attending his gigs. Their dates also consisted of them sightseeing, driving up the coast to see the foliage in Massachusetts, and Cape Cod. Adventurous right?! Richard recalls, *"Althea didn't sing with me often because she was snooty."* He played jazz, and she was a classical singer.

"Blacks in white neighborhoods had to know how to fight." Richard recalls. *"Otherwise, white people would just continuously disrespect you."* There was a family named The Clark's (Clahks) who lived above us. This family was known to be tough, and we had to be tougher. Richard's mother gave the discipline, and to show him how tough she was, she put on the boxing gloves and knocked Cecil against the door. Richard recalls a quick memory as to why he ended up being a gruff at times: *"My mouth got me into trouble a lot growing up. This brought about many butt whoopins for talking back to my mother."*

There was a time when Richard was about to get a whoopin', and he thought he could outrun his mother so he wouldn't get hit, but his mother ran faster than he thought! She was on his heels whoopin his butt all the way down the street! *"She didn't take no mess from anyone!"* Richard says. His parents never owned a home, but they wanted to. The Clarks ended up buying the house

Part I: The Man

his family lived in. The Clark's lived on the second and third floors, and The Reid's lived on the first floor. The rent was not free, and it continued to increase so when Richard got out of the military, he bought a two-story house of his own. He rented the first floor and lived on the second floor.

When Richard married Althea, he sold the house and moved to California. His brother Bobby was living in California and Althea had a cousin named Anne living there as well. The house The Reid's currently live in was purchased in June of 1978. Richard was working for Aretha Franklin then, and H.B. Barnum hired him. He connected with some well-known people. Jack Hahn was a music teacher in Watertown. He worked constantly, and Richard was his main bass player. If he couldn't get Reid, he didn't want another bass player. Richard was able to make good money. He played gigs that had only white band members. *"There were times when Jack Hahn, a white man, had to straighten suckas out because I was hired to play on a gig."* Richard says. Many owners didn't want a black bass player. Jack told Richard, *"I got a lot of static by putting you on a gig, but I told them if he can't play, you don't need me to play. He's my bass player. Period."* As Richard remembers his friend Jack and all he had done for Richard, he gets very emotional. He remembers being in downtown Boston and a strange male said something to Althea. Richard went out to find this man to "speak with him." Jack followed behind Richard to have his back. *"I never knew a white man would support me like that."* Richard says.

Because of his new connections, Richard was able to play throughout Massachusetts, and other jazz gigs with Alan Dawson before he came to California. Jack wasn't getting as many gigs with country clubs because they were cutting back, and Alan Dawson, a black man, was the top drum teacher at Berkeley School of Music so he often used Richard on many of his gigs. If anyone came into Boston to play who were from The Jazz Workshop, they would call Alan. Richard played for a lot of different musicians because of him.

It was difficult for Richard to reflect on the days of Jack Hahn, the one white man who believed in him and gave him a chance, and Alan Dawson. In a time when black men were not respected, he received his due publicly and privately. Being reminded of the racism he faced and the hard roads he traveled to get to where he is, though now he can celebrate, caused many tears to flow. Richard continues to share how difficult it was for him in the days of Jack Hahn, and another man named Alan Dawson, two men who'd paved the way for him. *"In a time when black men were not respected, he received his due publicly and privately because of them."* Richard says. More tears began to flow as he takes in those moments. He is reminded by his wife, Althea, that *"God placed white men in his life to add value. There were those in the military who wanted to take his stripes for his arrogance, but another white guy fought for him to keep them."* Althea says. *"Taking his stripes was meant to bring him down. When this was revealed, a white man transferred him to another unit. We cannot discredit those things, and not be angry at all white men. For every negative there was a positive. There can be anger, and when it's wrong is when it's outweighed to this point. Everyone has been mistreated. How do we handle that?"* Althea asks. *"We can either succumb to it or say all whites are like that, but they can say the same about us. How will we be any different?"* Richard says. *"There are people that spared him and gave him gifts. Jack Hahn pushed him through doors that he would have never gotten through at that time. Don't discredit how God used him to elevate you. It was a process. The realism is, he had to fight for that freedom. They didn't want to give it to him."* Althea says determinately.

"When they brought us here, (meaning slaves) it wasn't in the plan for us to be free. The handwriting was on the wall with His favor, even when Richard was born. He lost three siblings before he was born. In those same perilous times, God's hand was on his life. Despite all that happened, he is still here. Alan had a name, and whoever Alan sanctioned they went along with it. He picked Richard. Then Richard networked with more of them. This is another time to see God's favor on his life." Althea adds. *"When Richard came to California, he was already a known musician from Boston, and more gigs opened up since those establishments and connections were present. Richard played in the Parisian Room in Los Angeles. When he came here, he had already played with them in the past; Milt Jackson, Joe Williams, and other top*

Part I: The Man

jazz musicians to name a few. All of this helped the transition. Joe Williams told Red Holloway, the contractor, to use Richard Reid. Red had no idea. Joe pushed him to use Richard and worked with him until he died." Althea says. *"Big name singers and musicians played with him in the Parisian Room."*

Richard encourages and brings forth new musicians in how he introduces them and bring them to the worship services in having them participate in the Christmas Cantata. To them, it is not a big deal, but will impact them for the rest of their lives. Richard is doing for other musicians what Jack, Alan, and Joe did for him. He brings in quality musicians, and though we cannot pay them the value of their worth, they are bringing what is asked of them to this musical. Many of them have played for high-profile television shows. Nolan Shaheed was the one that got him the gig with Aretha Franklin. Nolan was connected with The Aretha Show, and H.B. Barnum was her music director. Nolan introduced Richard to H.B. in 1978. Richard was hired on a local gig to see how he played. He noticed Richard played the upright and Fender. After H.B saw what he was capable of, Richard was permanently on the road with Aretha. When he was hired to work with Aretha Franklin, H.B. Barnum wanted Richard to bring his upright bass. Richard mentioned that he needed a particular type of case to ship his instrument in. The argument from Management was, the container provided was sufficient, but Richard argued that it was not. Richard said, *"If you want me to take my upright, then you're gonna have to pay for a special case to be made and for the cost to ship it."* The management team reluctantly agreed to pay for shipping, and they also paid for the case to be made. The crazy thing is, *"I played at The Rose Bowl with it only one time."* Richard says while shaking his head. *"Probably because of what it cost to keep taking it on the road."* By paying for all of these special requests it showed that H.B. really wanted Richard to play for Aretha.

PART II, THE MUSIC (Minuet)
Tributes & The Family Portrait
"Slow, graceful, and often in 3/4 or 6/8 time"

"Family Portrait" was released in 2003. It is a tribute to Richard Reid's Family, and his heritage of Barbados. Track 1: "*Barbados Mir*"; Track 2: "*Three for Al*" is dedicated to his wife Althea Ellis Reid. Track 3: *"Dearing Dar"* is dedicated to his

Part II: The Music

fearlessly daring son, Darius, with Track 4: *"No I Mad"* dedicated to his first-born son who is the initial soundtrack to the family, Damion. It is clear Richard Reid keeps family first. Throughout his career, his heart is displayed in each stroke, each pluck, and each grunt as well as each tap of his foot.

This album was released in 2009. Richard A. Reid, Bassist, is a graduate of the New England Conservatory of Music. He has played with most of the top Jazz artists in the business. Richard Reid is a well-known and respected musician in the Jazz field. This CD tells the listener just what Richard is about.

Tributes

Damion Reid

MY INTERVIEW WITH DAMION, the eldest son of Richard and Althea, is via Zoom. He is walking around the backyard on a beautiful, summer afternoon. His earliest memory of his father is when he was around the age of three. This is when Damion began learning to play with ensembles as a drummer. He was taught lessons about life, responsibilities on the bandstand as well as the concept of family, fatherhood, and motherhood, and differentiating the relationships between the two. *"My father was the disciplinarian, but my mom had a lot of input, and was the neutralizer to keep things moving forward."* Damion says. *"My dad had a lot of principles and was stern at times. All of this was mixed in with life and I realized music was fun, but I had a responsibility, and I learned early to respect that, and to respect him."*

"*I was drawn to the drums naturally, and I was able to keep time at an early age. My dad bought me a drum set, but I tore it up. My parents bought me another one at the age of three, and I kept that set until I turned 11 years old. After that, my dad bought me a professional-grade set. My parents engrained musicality in me. It was never forced, and I was told it's fun, but it's also serious. "You will be held accountable."* My father would say. *"When I was in junior high, I became disenchanted with the drums. I was interested in manhood, girls, and other things. By the time I turned 14, the passion for the drums returned, and I couldn't stop thinking about it."* He remembers.

Part II: The Music

"*Before Darius was born, I remember the house being in disarray because my parents were adding on to the house. I saw my dad carrying lots of lumber, and I remember the smells as well. These memories are vivid in my mind.*" Damion shares. "*I used to hang on to my dad's leg while holding on to my mom. My dad helped me build my first car, an MGBGT. He used this car to show me how to do a few things mechanically, and at the age of 16, I ended up with a Cougar, a car that housed 390 horses under the hood. That was a lot of power for a kid.*" Damion laughs. "*I had to learn to drive on a stick shift, a manual car. I also had to get it painted. My father has an engineering degree, and with that background he knows how to take things apart, do modifications, and puts them back together. I was able to use those skills to work on a classic drum set Billy Higgins gave me. I had to take it apart completely, clean each component, and put it back together, and it became a coveted set. My dad is a thorough handyman. If he couldn't fix it, he'd bring in help, but not often.*"

"What is the one "thing" you and your father have that is all your own?"

"*Our thing was playing music. This is one of the biggest things that bonded us. Though my mother was a music teacher, she had more of a strict, written music, verbatim style. My dad played music verbatim as well, but he expounded on it which is another level, and those chops help you play rock and roll and jazz.*" Damion says. "*When I would get approval from his colleagues who happen to be world class, famous musicians, it became solidified for me. I collaborated with my father on both his CD's. I played the last track on his first album and Billy Higgins played the drums on the whole album. Billy also played the timbales, and I played the drums.*" He states fondly. "*On the second album, I played drums on all of them, and my father did different renditions. Even though I was away from the home in college, my father was able to document my maturation in music.*"

Damion reflects on what his father went through as a black man back in his day, and now, with the unsettling events during the pandemic and how he is to respond since both he and his brother Darius are connected in the white community.

Richard A Reid: The Man, The Music, and His Ministry

"*Through school, I was able to connect because h my father is multi-cultural. He demanded respect and the truth of what history has shown in his culture of African American and West Indian. He has never detached himself, and he didn't validate the behavior. He believed in working hard for what you want and not make excuses for not getting it. People have often tried to isolate us as black men to say we're only capable of certain things.*" Damion says.

"*The military and music took him around the world, and he made friends with Japanese, Italian, Irish, Jewish, West Indian, and African American men who were all musicians.*" He stated. "*Each year, when we'd visit the East coast, I saw diversity in my father's core group. He always treated people with respect and expected the same. His demeanor was logical.* "The minute someone crosses the line and tries to demean you for who you are and where you come from prejudging you, you have the right to "check" them." My father said. "*Him feeling the need to put us in the suburbs where it would be easier to educate us and take care of us giving us a different life from Cambridge, Massachusetts; those areas are rough.*"

"*He was unapologetic about his stance with teachers and other educators. Even though I have friends and collaborators who are not black, and some are West Indian, in my interactions, people can tell I was raised by someone who is West Indian. I tell them my father is Bajan. Deep down, he knows that no matter how successful a black person becomes, the level of stress will always be harder than it is for a white person. As I've gotten older, culturally, I understand why he is the way he is. My mother had more of the southern experience so there's a classic, Black American experience I get from her. My father also didn't want to seem narrow-minded. He taught us to use chopsticks and to learn other cultures; to learn their customs. He was always open to this and told my brother and I not to formulate an opinion until you taste something different.*"

Richard's family came from one environment, and he raised his children in another environment. That is how he was able to make it where he is now. "He made sure we knew who we were, instilling pride in us, and making sure we knew about what was

Part II: The Music

going on in the world." Damion says. *"Out of all my black friends, their parents never made us sit down to watch a documentary about Malcolm X, or Dr. Martin Luther King, Jr on television. This is who my father was. He also made me watch videos of great drummers. He wanted me to know myself and the impact our people have had on the planet."* My father said, *"If you have friends from other cultures who know and recognize that impact, those will be the friends you stick with, and don't worry about what culture they're from."*

"If you had to choose one superhero to compare your father to, his or her characteristics who would it be?"

"I would choose Wolverine from "The X-Men." Damion answers. *"He has the ability to be Hulk, and even though he has a mechanical mind and he's creative, he's more like Wolverine. Wolverine had healing powers, and he lived through many different time periods. He was also misunderstood and very cultured, but intolerant of the Tom Foolery. He is more skilled than people give him credit for, but he's cantankerous and probably wants to be left alone most of the time."* Damion says. *"Wolverine had a "staple" motorcycle, and my dad had the muscle car. The way Wolverine loved his motorcycle, my dad loved his cars. He was rugged around the edges and lived through wars. He keeps coming back no matter what, and people really shouldn't test him. I've seen other men confront my father, and it gets figured out quickly because others don't want things to escalate with him."*

"Watching my parents' relationship while growing up, my father was very grateful and happy about his decision of meeting and marrying my mother. Admiringly, he gives her credit for him still being alive, being the best thing to happen to him, and I want the same things in a wife, the trust, the dedication, and the love." Damion states. *"He would never do anything to mess that up."*

"In the world, he was in with the Marines, and the music and with all the spoils that were around, he chose to be at home with us. All couples go through their own stuff, but the main thing I pull from that is they forged together with the commitment and covenant to one another for nearly 50 years, to keep one another happy and watch each other die, and that's something to celebrate. They proved to me that it's tangible. It's special." He says with

sincerity. *"This is why my father worked so hard. Even after I wrecked my car, I was put on punishment, but he got me another one. Yes, you can make mistakes, but you deserve to learn from it and live after it."*

"When I got older, our relationship changed for the better. Initially, it was constant critique and scrutiny from my father, but it changed because he could see what I was accomplishing and how I was respected by his peers. They'd call him and give feedback unbeknownst to me and he respected the fact that I made a name for myself, and I was not solely leaning on him and his name to make it." Damion says. *"When people found out I was his son, there was a jolt in that community that favored me because of him. My father wanted to be free, free to do what he loved."*

While finishing up this interview, Damion gets distracted by a flying grasshopper. We discuss how he and Darius used to catch them when they were little, place them in jars, and then poke holes in the lid so the grasshoppers can breathe. Referring to the grasshoppers he states, *"Eventually, they'll die because they can't live in the jar for too long.". "But they want to be free. Free to do what they designed to do."*

"Is there anything you would like to say to your father as a last sentiment for this book?

"I want to say thank you for nurturing me and for choosing me when you could have chosen yourself. You chose to be selfless and hopefully, you'll be able to enjoy the remainder of your life. My brother and I can do so because he made sacrifices. I'm grateful he was so strict in the beginning because that gave me a skillset in a particular category that keeps me working. When my name comes up in crowds it's about the work ethic and my professional style. All of that comes from my dad giving me accountability at an early age." Damion said.

My dad would say, *"If you're on the stage and you're working, you need to be held accountable as someone who works. Don't think because you're a kid you can slide." "When I got whoopins, they were epic!"* He reflects. *"That's because I had done something really, really wrong. If my mother had to tell my dad, he was livid. There was a fear of getting in trouble with my father. If my mom, my aunts, or grandmother caught me slippin',*

Part II: The Music

hell fire came down on my head. I got taps, smacks, and licks from a belt, but they were memorable. He didn't like giving us whoopins. But he'd rather do that than to pick us up from the police precinct or other venue such as that one, and obviously, they worked. I attended a Catholic school, and they were disciplined as well." Damion says.

"How have things been since being home during the pandemic?"

"Being home during the pandemic at our age, my brother and I were intentional about making sure our parents were healthy and happy. We could've stayed on the East coast and stress out, but we came together as a family. Most parents are placed in homes while their children move on without them, but this is a hard time in our history, and it worked out perfectly. I was able to rekindle my relationship with my parents because while living on the East coast, I wasn't able to come home as often as my brother. Once we were locked down, we were able to get clarity on what needed to be done. It also took a weight off my mother's shoulders because her boys are here to assist her and our father. If we were married with children, those responsibilities would have taken precedent. I haven't been home this long since I was 18 years old. It's been nostalgic being home, but it was all about putting family first as we were taught."

"Are there any final words you would like to share with your father?"

"Thank you for taking the time to teach me life lessons and how to take care of myself in multiple situations, whether it was about taking care of a family or my finances. A lot of people didn't have the same type of father-figure. Most of my friends have "dads." A real Father shows you how to be accountable, how to be responsible, how to figure out life and its passion, your life work, and to find satisfaction in it. No one wants to see their kid struggle." Damion says. My father would say, *"Love what you do, and do what you love, work hard at it, and don't make excuses." "In the last five years, I have been able to see the benefits from his discipline, and he can poke his chest out because of it. He didn't have to do it, but I'm grateful he did."*

Darius Reid

IN THE BEGINNING OF OUR INTERVIEW, Darius is deep in thought while remembering the early days with his father. He laughs to himself as if the memory that quickly popped into his head still rings true as if it were yesterday.

"I don't remember the different ages of when I had these encounters, but I do recall these things." Darius says.

"When I was a kid, my father brought discipline from day one; nipping things in the bud that I would do; instilling in me the pride of who I was then, who I would become as a man, a black man." Darius said.

"What kind of things?"

"Things like walking with my head above my shoulders, no slouching. He would make me stand against the wall for 15 minutes, and say, "You don't slouch. You walk with your head held high." That was the start of everything. "There was a lot of discipline. He taught me that can't isn't a word. There's nothing I cannot do. I just have to do it. A lot of his thoughts were through will power, and then as I got older, there was a way to make that fit strategically. Much of my foundation came from that as well as him being a force of intimidation. This was his entire M.O. I was a bad kid!" Darius remembers "I bent the rules often and challenged the system. I would get a lot of whoopin's in public, and he would dare anyone to say something about it. Bad or misguided behavior was not tolerated. Whether it was through physical discipline or any other means, it guided me quickly."

As I continue to talk with Darius, each memory that resurfaces causes him to laugh heartily and his shoulders soften as he thinks back on the lessons his father taught him and his brother Damion.

"My father always told us that we could do anything. He was very hands on. We would change oil and filters in a bunch of cars. I hated that!" Darius said. "I don't know if he knew that the lessons he taught showed us how to be self-sustaining. We wanted a playhouse, so we had to help build it." My father said, "If you want something, you're going to have to put forth the effort and build it yourself." "Not knowing that may have been what he wanted us to do instead of just asking and it appears. Otherwise, we'd get

Part II: The Music

accustomed to this lifestyle which is called the "silver spoon mentality." He also taught us to put shingles down for roofing. That wasn't my expertise." Darius admits. *"I vowed never to use my hands for that type of work as a profession. I told myself when I got older, I am going to sit behind a desk and boss people around."*

"When I was about six or seven years old, my father enrolled me in martial arts as a way of gaining discipline, and to help me control my temper; It's probably the island in me." Darius says. *"The martial arts and other disciplines, those things helped mold me into the person I am today. This is a good thing, and it sparked the competitive part of me; to be strategic, and precise; to be intentional about it. It's a metaphor for deflecting and blocking. Strong seeds were planted early on."*

"I heard you play the piano. How did that come about?"

"I began playing piano at an early age. Initially, I wanted to play the bass like my dad, but my father said, "You don't play the bass. I play the bass." *I disagreed with him."* Darius said. *"He was adamant in creating the "family band" with him on Bass, my brother on drums, me on piano, and my mom on vocals, but this wasn't what I wanted to do."* Darius protested. *"My mother was instrumental in nurturing me in playing piano, and there were a lot of lessons learned in it. The piano was the instrument of choice in the house."*

"My dad is not a "nugget dropper" he's a reactor." Darius added. *"When I would act up in school, he would just "appear."* He would let it be known to me that "We're gonna have a session when we get home." *"This meant a butt whoopin' was comin'. He taught us for every action there is a reaction or consequence. I was always testy. He would just be in the doorway after he received the message that I was acting up in school. I would lie on the bed and get that belt on my butt. It was raw, but it wasn't child abuse."* Darius confirms. *"It was never us sitting down and we have conversation like you see men sitting on a bench in a park. That wasn't his style. The Reid household was a butt whoopin' house. If I tried to block a hit, I would get another hit because I tried to block it. My mother played more of the "Hallmark movie" role, but if I messed up, I knew that I would have to deal with my father*

when he got home. He played the enforcer role. I didn't learn at first, but it came later as I began to use more critical thinking. It created a toughness in me."

"My father was intentional about grooming us as young, black men, and when he saw we were becoming adults, the conversations changed." Darius remembers.

"What do you mean it changed? How?"

"My father taught us about things to do or not do when getting pulled over by law enforcement; how to conduct ourselves in not making sudden moves, having information quickly accessible, being and staying non-confrontational because there's probably already some doubt there." Darius says. "There were never words used like profiling or biases, but that does come about right away. These things helped us to live to fight another day or get out of that situation without losing our lives because of another weak human being. The discipline and effort we have to give is gonna have to be different because we aren't viewed as an equal; not right or wrong, but that is the reality. It was always in the background because of the lessons he taught us early on."

"What are some memories of you and Damion that you can share?" I asked.

"Me and my brother's first cars were stick-shifts. This was non-negotiable. We had to learn how to drive a manual car; to control an engine and understand if you're going to be using something, know what it takes for upkeep." He says. "I learned what was happening when shifting gears. These were guys' type stuff we discussed, but he was intentional. We learned about what it took to take care of a car and what happens with the engine when you rev it up." Darius says. "These were lessons we could apply to life in general; understanding what it takes to shift. We manually control it. In essence, we take ownership of what we've done. It taught me to know my input, and to create the output I wanted. It's a great life lesson."

"Why do you call your father Superman?"

"As a child, I reflect on why I call my father Superman. This is because I felt there wasn't anything he couldn't handle, or anything he couldn't do. Anything that needed to be done got done. He adapted to any task. He had that willpower." Darius says.

Part II: The Music

"After I left the nest, I didn't come back. I was that bird that just flew away. In adulthood, I was who I was, but there was never anything I couldn't ask him for if I needed it. There was a time when I was attending Pasadena City College, I had a coach that was racist. My dad went to the school, confronted him, and then took him to the mark." Darius reflects. *"The coach ended up getting fired. This was a "superhero" moment! He got the justice that was needed. My father would do this with anyone."* *"Now that I am a grown man our conversations are minimal, but it doesn't have to be full of a lot of words for us to talk. He fusses more now."* Darius laughs. *"There's more conversation with my mother because that's the nature of it. He is not a talkative man. Never has been, never will be. He has a lot of proud moments concerning me that he finds out through other people."*

"Do you feel you and your father are on leveled ground now, and if they can talk to one another like men?"

"He has more of an awe of what has transpired; watching his seeds grow and come to life." Darius says of his father. *"Dad is more of a "sit back and watch" and doesn't articulate what he means. His facial expressions are known throughout the family. He nods if it's good. No nod, it's not good. His strokes are very broad. Like, he won't say, "Hey Darius, do you wanna go to the store?" It was more like, "Let's go to the store", but I never knew where we were going. This was his way of bonding."*

"A good example of this is we drove an hour to Dairy Queen to get ice cream. It was his way of spending quality time with me. No conversation, just the 88.1 radio station blaring. This was his way of letting me into his world. I was often his road dog because we are a lot alike. We fixed things together, not a lot of talking, but a lot of doing" Darius said. *"Though he'd want it done his way, the wrong way, this is where the precious moments were created.*

"How does it make you feel knowing your father is a Living Legend in the Jazz and R&B world?"

"It is a proud moment for me for sure knowing he has been acknowledged for his body of work in music. It was a cool thing to see transpire when I was a child, and now as an adult. This is something that will live on through the family legacy because it

sets an example for generations to come; the people with whom he was acknowledged."

"Is there anything you want to say as a lasting memory for this book?"

"*In closing, I want to say thank you to my dad for being there and being present. Even when he didn't know how to articulate it, it mattered, and it went a long way.*" Darius says with a slight choke in his voice. "*He didn't have to be there. It's sad to say, but a majority of black men weren't around, and he was. He made an active decision to be there and be the provider. He made the Reid name proud. He would always tell me, "You're a Reid!" That matters, and it's a big deal, and those things I take out into the world today. I use these things in my business practices; discipline and staying the course is applied to everything I do.*" Darius says.

"*There is no magic formula. The road will get dark, but there is light, but you must push through; this is what I've always seen my dad do; push through. His willpower is on a different level. One last example of him being on a higher level is, every holiday he would hand deliver and hand write thank you notes to people who had done things for him. He never took people for granted. He always took time out to make it real to others.*"

Henry (Shack) and Tayja Mashack - Family

DURING OUR INTERVIEW, The Mashack's have taken time out of their "Family Fun Day" to do this interview with me. It was in the late 1980's, and Tayja and Henry, nicknamed Shack, attended the same church as The Reid's. Tayja's mom had just passed away, and with another event, a great number of church members were returning from a trip in New Mexico. Both Tayja and Shack realized they needed more fulfillment than what they were receiving at their current place of worship. They lived not far from St. Stephen Baptist Church, and Shack had gone by the church a few times. When they purchased their home in Pomona, they decided to give St. Stephen a try. While speaking to Tayja, her son, Brandon, enters with *his* son Braylon. Their granddaughter, Justice, also decided to join the Zoom call. With a smile on her face, Brandon's wife, Connie, joins in and comments on the Dallas Cowboy jersey I am wearing. He also comments that I don't know any better. We all laugh at the truth and continue with the interview.

Shack and Tayja joined one of the choirs and they connected with Althea and Richard immediately. The Mashack boys were also in the same Sunday school class as Richard and Althea's, and they attended the same school as well. When the Mashack's and Reid's found out whose children belonged to whom, they both knew their children were safe.

Shack remembers Althea walking up to him and saying, *"You remind me of my husband. You need to meet my husband."* Shack agreed. The Mashack's were invited over to the Reid's home for dinner where he and Richard hit it off immediately. *"We are the best of friends."* Shack states. *"Out of all the buddies I've known, Richard is it."* Shack says. "We shared everything about our lives from their military experiences, the streetlights coming on, and to Shack being a gang member. *"Richard didn't join a gang, although he was close to doing so."* Shack says. Shack often thought he was older than Richard, but when Richard would spout off at the mouth, Shack would jump in his chest really quick. Althea took notice to that. "I thought Richard listened to me because I was older, but Althea corrected him and said, *"Richard was the oldest of the two."*

Tayja entertains her grandson while speaking with me. The two of them are very involved in their adult children and grandchildren's lives. Before they had a chance to answer, Brandon interjects from behind the scenes. Tayja speaks of a time when they asked Richard and Althea to go with them to Pismo Beach on vacation. *"All of us crammed into the motor home and hung out for a full week."* Tayja said. *"A tent was created outside the motor home for the young men to sleep in. Video games were brought, and an entrance and exit to come in to eat and use the facilities and go back out was created."* Richard mentioned to Shack that he wanted to ride the Dune Buggies since he saw some other guys doing so. Richard said, *"We'll just take some from the guys and if the police come, we'll dump them before they catch us."* Shack laughs. *"Richard never acted on this thought."* They took many day trips with both their families and packed the coolers with lunch and other snacks. *"We visited places like Magic Mountain, Big Bear, and Universal Studios. Foods like spaghetti, salad, bread, and hot dogs were kept in the motor home."* Tayja said. *"Each kid was given $10 to spend in the amusement park, and if they ran out of money, they were out of luck until they came out of the park."* Shack mentioned. *"The boys often took a football to throw around while they waited in line. A curfew was given before they left, and a head count was done before they entered the park, and after the came out."* Tayja said. *"Our relationship was more organic. Of course, God was in it, but we connected naturally. There were times when each of us took the kids for a week at a time in the Summer. This was to give everyone a break."* Shack said.

Tayja mentions, *"During the school year when it was time for finals, all the kids stayed at the Reid's house. Richard was not working outside the home at the time, and he made sure the kids were prepared for their finals. They knew going over to the Reid's home meant they would study and not mess around because Richard didn't allow it."* Since their kids attended the same high school, Richard was there for them when The Mashack's son, Elton, broke his wrist. Richard just told the doctors to go ahead and do the surgery.

Part II: The Music

A memory shared by Shack is, *"One requirement of the school for the parents was they had to serve a number of volunteer hours either at games, booster club meetings, or other student events. Richard made arrangements with the school administration for other parents who were not available because of their work schedules, and the school allowed Richard to cover each of their shifts as needed. This was a relief. Richard was just that kind of guy."* Tayja said. *"We could always count on him."*

"There was a time our minivan was part of an accident while parked on the street. We had to get a rental car while our vehicle was being repaired." Tayja said. *"On this particular day, I was scheduled to pick up the kids from school and take them to the church. Someone, then, hit the rental car, and the driver of the car who hit the rental car was arguing and would not give his driver's license to me."* Tayja continues. *"I saw Richard pass by, and I yelled out his name. Richard turned his car around to come to where I was. I told him what happened."* Richard said to the man, *"Listen sucka! I need you to give her your ID so she can file her claim. Plus, I gotta go to the bathroom so I need you to hurry up!"* Tayja laughs. *"Richard was already taking his belt off whenthe other driver stated he could fix the car for Tayja so she wouldn't have to turn it in damaged."* Richard told the man that if it wasn't done correctly, he would come find him." Tayja added. *"The repairs were done correctly, and they didn't have to take the car in."*

Shack tells a story about attending a gig with Richard in Palm Springs. *"During the sound check, Richard walked in late. The band gave him a rip about it, and Richard grumbled."* Shack said. *"Someone in the band asked,* "Who is that with you?" *"Richard would tell the band that I was his bodyguard."* Shack said. *"I whipped my jacket back so they'd see my gun and said,* "I'll kill everybody in here!" *"The guys got so scared, but me and Richard laughed. The band members apologized repeatedly to Richard."*

"There was another time someone plugged their cord into Richard's amp while they were doing a sound check in San Diego." Shack said. *"It was someone from another group. Richard almost turned the place out! He does not like anyone touching his stuff!"* Any time he wanted to go somewhere, he'd call Shack and say,

"Shack, let's go somewhere." *"He's always got a million things to do."* Tayja said. *"He always wanted a discount when he shopped."* Shack shared. *"If they didn't give him the right price, he'd say,* "Alright sucka, if I don't get what I want I'll put Shack on you." We would laugh so hard at their reaction

Both Tayja and Shack could be with Althea and Richard for weeks at a time, and they never got tired of one another. Their kids enjoyed being with one another as well. Their relationship continued to grow because they all loved being together. Althea and Shack often shared sarcastic comments between them. Althea knew what buttons to push to make Shack mad, and it just continued as they got older. *"I remember making the "Mission", a school project for Darius."* Tayja said. *"That project was used for three different kids. All of them received an "A" on the project. Thankfully, they attended three different schools, and the teachers never knew."* She continued. *"It didn't take much for all of us to be happy. We could do a staycation and be together. The kids didn't care either."* It was then that their daughter, Danielle, became Althea and Richard's daughter since she was the only girl in the group of kids.

"When Richard turned 70, Danielle flew in for his birthday celebration. This melted his heart." Tayja said. *"There were things Richard shared with just Brandon, and this is how they bonded."* Shack said. *"Richard felt the kids should have a job to do on Saturdays. They couldn't just stay in bed or sit around watching television all day. He made Brandon sweep the leaves off the roof.* When Althea saw this, she yelled, "If you don't get my baby down off the roof!" Brandon was told to get down immediately! *"Some of the other kids were cleaning the car, washing dishes, and picking up trash. He was a tyrant to some degree and felt everyone had to have an assignment."* Shack said. *"When we went to the Mashack's we didn't have to work on Saturdays."* Brandon interjects. *"If someone helped the kids with their chores, Richard would come behind them and redo what they've done. His military disciplines kicked in."* Tayja said to Richard, *"Let me tell you this so there's no misunderstanding. I will never clean for you again."* We'll just go to breakfast." Richard said, *"That's fine."* I replied, and he kept cleaning.

Part II: The Music

Shack remembers Richard trying to clamp his hand down with his famous handshake. Since Shack was in the gym daily at that time, when they locked hands, Shack's grip got tighter and tighter and so did Richard's. Richard tried to break him down, but he couldn't. "*Man, most people be on the floor by now, but I can't get you down.*" Richard said. "*Never forget that!*" Shack said. They laughed. "*Shack tries to warn people about the handshake because Richard's hand will crush you.*" Tayja said.

"Are there any character traits about Richard you would like to share?"

"*Some character traits Richard has passed on is he is extremely loyal. He believes in family and doing what's right. He has crazy ideas, but he's always genuine in all he does. He's never phony. He doesn't talk behind your back. If he's got something to say, he'll say it to your face.*" Shack says. "*We both told our boys what a man does and how he should carry himself in life, how they should live. We stuck together in showing our boys how to be men. I couldn't ask for a more devoted friend.*" "*When Richard and Althea bought a timeshare, they didn't want to go unless we went with them.*" Tayja said. "Tayja and I agreed to go with them each time. While there, we decided that, "This is *our* timeshare." "*When we bought ours in Hawaii, we said the same thing to them.*" Tayja said. "*Anytime we go to Hawaii, they're always with us. Everywhere we go, they normally go, and it goes both ways. We plan most of our trips together.*" "*Tayja and Althea do all the planning.*" Shack said. "*Richard and Shack do the packing.*" Tayja said. "*Really, the ladies just tell us what to do.*" Shack said.

Tayja shares a reflection on Richard as well. "*Though Richard has a roar, when you really get to know him, he's very compassionate. You have to be in that space for him; you've proven who you are. I can speak for our family when I say there isn't anything he wouldn't do to make sure our family is okay. I can call him right now and he'd figure out how to make it happen. Most people don't see it because his roar keeps people away.*" They both laugh. "*Richard and I have a love relationship that has its battles. I'll tell him he doesn't know what he's talking about, and then instead of eating humble pie, Richard will say he checked with someone else, and they said I might be right. That's just him." She laughs.

"I've told him several times not to go head-to-head with me about things I know well. The last time we went on a trip, we took our car to my son's house to leave it there. Richard and Althea were following us. Richard comes up to the side of me and tells me I'm going the wrong way." Tayja shares. Shack says to Richard, "You know she's not gonna follow you." They laugh and keep driving. After arriving at Tayja's son's house, Richard decides he will drive, but Tayja doesn't want him to. "Richard just completed his hip replacement surgery and had not driven in months." Tayja said. "Tayja told him to pull over because she was not going to ride with him." Shack said. "Though he gave her a grunt, he stopped the car and allowed Shack to drive. Richard wants to be in control, and no one is allowing him to be." Tayja laughs.

"Is there anything else you would like to share?"

"We will always be there for our friends, Althea and Richard. They never have to wonder or ask. All they have to say is they need us and we're on our way." Shack says. "This is a priceless relationship to have. Regardless of what happens, knowing someone has you is a valuable thing. They don't come in asking a lot of questions, they just ask how can we help? In the spaces of time when we've needed them, they were there. They've seen the good, the bad, and the ugly while raising our children and in our marriage." Tayja says.

"Althea was able to gain my trust because she proved herself to be that girl." Tayja adds. "We just want them to know, we got you! Whatever it is." "When each of our parents and siblings passed away, we were there for one another." Shack says. We even held up my dad's funeral so Damion could attend." Tayja mentions. "We all respected the parents and grandparents as if they were ours. On both sides, all are adoringly named Auntie, Uncle, Granddad, Grandma, and Boom Boom." Tayja says. Shack mentions that he doesn't call a lot of people his friend. He states he and Richard can read each other without words. "We know each other. That's how we are. I'd give my life for him. That's how close we are, and other people notice that as well." Shack says. "All of us that served in Vietnam together are my brothers. Although

Part II: The Music

Richard never went to Vietnam, he's my brother. Richard is also very humble when he receives an honor. He doesn't feel he should be rewarded for being recognized for being a Living Legend." Shack continues. Shack tried not to cry, but he couldn't hold back his tears while talking about his friend and brother, Richard. *"He doesn't know how much he's loved."* Shack stated. *"He's such a wonderful person."*

Billy and Mimi Thompson — Family

BILLY AND RICHARD MET through their mutual occupation and profession of being a musician. While Billy played the saxophone, and Richard played the upright Bass, they became acquainted with one another. They actually grew up a couple cities apart. *"Most musicians of color played together, but they didn't segregate themselves to different cities. There were some musicians that both were familiar with, and Richard was well-known with a personality unlike anyone else, which is great!"* Billy says.

"When I think of Richard, I think of a "cool dude." Billy says. "What I mean is, he was loyal and courageous, good natured, highly intelligent, witty, gifted, artistic, and a dangerous man." Billy laughs. *"You don't want to be on the wrong side of Richard if you have a choice. I make these comments because I've known Richard for more than 40 years, and he would give me the shirt off his back if he felt it would save my life. He is a sincere musician, parent, and father image, and an excellent example of a "real friend" to me. This sums up who I think Richard is."* Billy continues. *"We were teens when we met. We had friends of various ethnic and age groups. I got to know my wife through Richard when he and Althea came to visit California. At that time, I was going through a divorce."* Billy says. *"Richard and Althea brought someone with them, a lovely woman who has since become my dear wife, Mimi. He is the kind of person you want on your team when all seems lost. He's a genuine and giving person. I can jokingly say a lot about him, and he's not a pretentious person. He has a lot of class, clout, and pride. His ethnic background extends to the West Indies and he's proud of his culture. He's noted by most all of the skilled musicians and artists in the Boston, Massachusetts area. We're good buddies, and we've become closer since we had so much in common."* Billy said. *"When I visited his home in California we'd enjoy one another's company, although I hadn't had the opportunity to do so lately* due to the pandemic."

"What was it like playing with Richard?"

"Any time I played a gig with Richard, they're all special because he's a special person. He's the one that makes the

Part II: The Music

difference between it being just a gig from an artistic point of view. He had all those qualities. He's a rare bird. He's also a perfectionist." Billy laughs. *"Whether it was the art, or things in his home, he wanted to improve those and things around him. We loved talking about automobiles. We challenged one another on who had the fastest car. He NEVER wanted to be second. It could be part of his background because West Indians have a lot of pride."* Billy said.

"I remember a time when Richard and I ran across one another on an open highway. He always had the latest and greatest of "hot cars." This time, I had the hottest car. We raced and I won because mine was the "baddest" and I came out ahead, but Richard will never admit it." Billy laughs as he recounts the story. Billy recalls random memories and says, *"I remember a time when we were headed to New York. I was driving and I attempted to pass a car. Unfortunately, I dozed off, or wasn't concentrating, and Richard grabbed the wheel to prevent us from having a very serious accident. He was always aware of things and people around him. Because of this, he saved our lives. When it came to speaking with people around the country, he didn't care whether you were black or white. Even though there were many challenges in those days, Richard treated everyone fairly and with respect. Richard gave me inspiration when he played, and it can depend on the instrument one plays. Musicians like myself, Johnny Hodges, Charlie Parker, Cold Train are who we consider to be pioneers in this game."* Billy shares.

"We can tell in how the way he runs his home and keeps up his property as well as how he has taught his sons, and the religious background, that he is who he says he is. When you have children, they follow your example. Richard showed this as opportunities presented themselves. One can't act the same as they did once you become a figure of authority. Both of us are the examples, the role models for them to follow." Mimi adds.

When speaking about Richard dating Althea, Billy says he doesn't know much. This is possibly to tame the reports a bit. *"Richard went through a few changes."* Billy says. *"He knew the "wild" Richard and saw what Althea did to "tame" him."*

"*Thank God for Althea!*" Mimi interjects with laughter. Mimi states, "*Richard is crazy!*"

"*When I met Althea and Richard, Althea was pregnant with Damion. Althea was sweet, but Richard was gruff and rough.*" Mimi said. "*Whenever they'd meet, she just had to punch him because she knew he had done something wrong. We used to vacation together, and Richard was like a big brother to me. Althea's mom used to tell many stories about how Richard protected his family. Richard barks at you.*" Boom Boom would say.

"*Once we were in Detroit and Richard was driving to come pick me up and Boom Boom, Althea's mother, was in the vehicle* Richard kept mouthing off, and Boom Boom said, "Listen here! I'll stop this car and put you out!" "*You don't play with Althea's mother. She said what she meant. After Boom Boom spoke, Richard never uttered another word!*" Mimi said. "*When I got into the car I asked,* "What happened?" Althea leaned over to me and said, "*Boom Boom spoke now everybody is quiet!*"

"*Richard is also one who does not sugar cote his words, but he's loving. He has your best interest at heart as far as what he sees in you. Richard is kind-hearted even though he has this rough exterior. He's a marshmallow, but not a pushover. He'll do anything for you if he likes you. If not, you'll have a hard road to hoe. And he doesn't hide it! He says what he means and means what he says. What you see is what you get.*" Mimi says. "*He's done the "handshake" with Billy more times than he cares to remember.*"

"*Nobody wants to get their hand shaken by Richard. He'll give you that look, take your hand, and then it's all over.*" Billy said.

"*Devil Dogs, Pearl Hot Dogs, and his Moxie. These are his Boston favorites.*" Mimi says. "*The Moxie is a drink in Massachusetts. Moxie was like a Pepsi, but had a slight therapeutic overtone to it, and Hermits (like a cookie) as well. Devil Dogs are like cookies that are long and dark with a fluff marshmallow in the middle.*"

"What is something you'd like people to know before we end this interview?"

Part II: The Music

"I would like people to know what we've already stated, "what you see is what you get." He likes to have fun, he like to laugh, and he's a man of God. That is the one thing that changed his life, his relationship with God and his relationship with Althea." Billy says.

"I would like to say that I thank God for Richard's kind heart. He will help you in any way that he can. He's for real, and you don't have to try to guess what he's thinking or how he feels. He is an open person and we're both glad we got to know him. When he walks into a room, you know it. He has shaped my life in so many ways." Mimi says. "Richard has a sense of humor because he was given Darius as a "little Richard." He is tough and tender, and very protective of me. It has been an honor to call him my family and my friend."

Beatrice "Bea" Johnson, Musician - Family Friend

BEA REMEMBERS MEETING RICHARD in 1989. She, Richard, and Althea attended the same church. At this time, Althea was the music director and Bea was already playing the organ for two choirs. After one of the services were over, Althea approached her and asked if she would consider adding another choir to her regimen. Bea agreed. The common thread in meeting Richard is that Althea is the segue, a bodyguard of sorts to everyone who met Richard in church.

"My first impression of Richard was that Richard knew his stuff. He knew his music. Not only did he know his stuff, but he knew everyone else's as well. This was important because he helped make her a better musician. He wasn't exactly gentle, and because he knew the music, he would often encourage me about what I "should" be playing on any given sheet of music. I remember him saying something like, "You're supposed to play a B-flat 9, minus chord in measure #26. I had never really played with anybody like him." Bea recalls. *"You know once he said that I was like uh-oh, I gotta practice a little more."*

"In rehearsals, sometimes, a musician can play through and learn as they go, and nobody would call you out or say those kinds of things. You can get by, or make sure you have it right the next time. No one usually said anything to me, but with Richard, I needed to have it the first time." She laughs. *"I appreciate him in that sense. When I was awarded the MIA award (Musicians in Action), I mentioned him in the video when I was interviewed. Each musician was asked about their careers in music and ministry, and those who had been instrumental in their lives. There were two that I mentioned, and one of them was Richard Reid. I really leaned on Richard a lot. I knew that if I could hear him, I knew where I was going and how I was supposed to do my chords. He was my crutch."* Bea said.

"What kind of work ethic would you say Richard has?"

"Richard is a perfectionist. When you've had the type of musical training and all the experience that he's had I wouldn't expect anything less. I didn't have formal training or experience. I am self-taught. I taught myself to play the organ. I took piano

Part II: The Music

lessons when I was a little girl and that was it. I started playing for the Sunday school and haven't had any training since." She laughs. *"If there was a music war, Richard Reid is who she would like in her fox hole for sure. We didn't do gigs together outside of church. I didn't do anything together with other musicians because you can't take the organ with you (smiles). I'm not the kind of musician that does gigs."* Bea says.

"Is Richard a name-dropper?"

"Richard has mentioned a few folks in the past; a little name-dropping though I can't remember who. He was not arrogant about it." Bea says.

"I've heard mention that a few musicians feared Richard because of his size and his gruff. What do you say?"

"Richard never scared me like others. He took me under his wing. I don't know how many other female musicians he's played with. It's usually men. He was never ever rough or gruff with me, but he was with the men especially as they prepared for a musical performance at church. He is not the kind of guy that holds back so you need to come prepared and know your part. He didn't take no mess! I have been in the room with him, and he never pulls any punches. Sometimes I wanna say, "don't be so cold." She laughs. *"He's a professional and a perfectionist. How about that!"* It is clear that Richard holds everything together. He doesn't need the support of the others in order to play. He feels he is doing his part and so should everyone else."

"How would you describe his family dynamics?"

"I remember when one of the main musicians at the church had left. I remember being unprepared mentally I was to cover for this musician. I would go to the Reid's home and go over some music together with Richard to get her prepared. I've never had that kind of experience before while working at any church." Bea says. *"Both Althea and Richard were more than willing to help me in any way as a musician and make the music ministry to be what it should be. I am forever grateful to both of them for that, and I want to make sure they get proper recognition."* She says.

"How does it feel to be working with a living legend?"

"Funny you should say that because that's what I call him. I call him Double L. He's had that nickname ever since she

witnessed his induction into the Living Legend Hall of Fame. Richard never mentions his status. He brags on his boys about where Damion is playing, or what Darius is doing in the professional world." Bea recalls.

"Are there any last sentiments you would like to share?"

"*I want to thank him for making me a better musician, and not in a pushy way. He's probably not aware of it, and he didn't go to the MIA's (Musicians In Action Awards) by the way (friendly jab), but in relation to him, it was the honor to play with him. I have two of his CD's and when I listen to him play, I am amazed! Gospel music is what it is, but when you hear him play the jazz stuff, it's amazing!*" Bea says. "*The musicianship really shines through. He is one-of-a-kind. It is truly and honor. Oh, I remember something funny he says after one of our church services, "Well, we fooled 'em again."* She laughs. "*For him to still be hangin' on is also amazing. I hear his grunting when he plays. He makes these noises. I don't know if it's timing, or he's playing his part in his head. He's always happy to see me, and that makes me feel comfortable. He's so special.*"

Dr. Anthony L. Dockery – Richard & Althea's Pastor

"How did you first meet Richard Reid?"

"I first met Brother Reid in 1990, here at St. Stephen Baptist Church by connecting with his sons, Damion and Darius. He was playing for the Chancel choir, but I met his wife first. He told me of how he met his wife; how he called her his Georgia Peach. I still tease her about that nickname to this day. All of this was in our first conversation. I was a fairly new minister, and I learned they were a musical family from Detroit." Dockery says. *"His wife attended Cass Technical High School, a special school which is by invitation only. I teased her because she was smart and gifted. Most of my conversations with him were short yet packed with information."* He recalls.

"I remember in the Fall and Winter, he'd wear a Buffalo Soldiers jacket which turned out to be another stimulus in our conversations. He wanted to learn about the history of them and it got my attention, so I asked him about it. We also had military life in common. I served in the Air Force, and he served as a Marine. Brother Reid teased me about my military life." He'd say, "Marines are tough, and the rest are weak." *"He was intrigued about my time in the Air Force and being a pilot and flying an airplane, and also the missions. There were times when he'd talk about the impacts of war, and his facial expression would change as he shared his life in the Marines. There aren't many guys who share their experiences, good or bad."* Dockery said. *"That was a special moment for me. Sometime later, we'd discuss his boys; how he raised them. The difference in they are different people in their aspirations, and how he is proud of them in their accomplishments. I cannot describe how proud he is of them. I had the opportunity to spend time with Damion and Darius in the youth department; going to conferences and watching them sing in the choir."* He recalls.

"Have you ever experienced one of his famous handshakes?"

"I remember his vice grips in the handshakes. As soon as I could, I would rip my hand away." Dockery says. *"We also talked about cars. He likes classics and he likes to drive very fast. We shared music as well. Brother Reid once told me he could tell I*

enjoyed music. "I can tell you get into music." Reid said to him. *"These are all things that endeared us to one another, those commonalities. I was more distant with Sis. Reid because of the choir, but once she was hired, I got to know her a little better. She often told me of how she has to hide foods he isn't supposed to have."* He laughs. *"I remember the classic, green, Scooby Doo van as well."*

"Brother Reid is not only a living legend in music, but he's a legend in his faith. His persona can come off as rugged or put-offish, but he's a gentle giant. He is compassionate Marine which you don't find very often. He really cares about people and want what's best for them. He will serve others. Now, he does not play, and he demands excellence. That's because he is excellent! He is not a musical living legend by happenstance. He put in the work and he's serious about it." Dockery says.

"Are there any last words you'd like to share?"

"I really appreciate him taking his faith seriously. That rounded him out and brought balance especially in this stage of life. I'm not saying he was a heathen or anything, but he became more studious about the Word. He would approach me afterwards and ask questions to get more answers. I've never known anyone to say they reached out to Richard Reid and he acted as if he didn't care." Dockery says. *"If anyone potentially got off on the wrong foot that's on them because he's a good guy. Yes, he can appear intimidating, but he's not. He is a Psalm 1 man and bass player who has earned the title of legend."*

Jeannie Cheatham, World Class Piano Player/Musician/Singer/Songwriter
A Family Friend

CHEATHAM IS A JAZZ PIANO PLAYER, but plays all kinds of music. She began playing at the age of six for her church. She played big and small bands, some solo piano, but didn't sing until later in life. She had the Sweet Baby Blues Band, and worked with Red Callendar. After Red died, Nolan Rasheed and Richard joined the band, and along with Charles Owens, Rickey Woodard, Louis Taylor, Herman Riley, and Marshal Hawkins formed the new Sweet Baby Blues Band. Chris Pegler, Jimmy, Noom, Dickey, Morris, and Red, Ironman Harris, and a girl trumpet player named Claire Bryant, and Ernie Fields, a contractor, all worked together in their career. Some of them took part in movies as well.

She nicknamed him "Rough House Reid" because he was a big man who often wore a big, black jacket and a black cap over his eyes. *"Sometimes these guys would mess around and joke with me a lot, or not be ready for gigs. This meant they didn't rehearse like they should have, and I would tell them, "If y'all don't act right ima have Richard fall on you and crush you!" We'd get a good laugh from all of it."* Jeannie says. *"Playing with Richard was a joy! He was never late to rehearsals or gigs. A lot of musicians don't do that. He always played in tune, and was attuned to vocalists, and that's a gift because a lot of musicians don't know how to do that. It's a little like physics. You gotta know your instrument and have an ear and a feel to it. Richard played at the neck of the upright bass. Sometimes, a vocalist has a lot of long notes, and he was unselfish. He played "with" the artist, not for the artist."* Jeannie states. *"He supported the singers and the rest of the band members in that way. Even trumpet players depended on him. Richard performed what is called a "walking bass." This is essential to the Kansas City style of music that we played. He has always been dependable."*

"When did you begin playing with Richard Reid?"

"We started playing in the early 1990's. To my knowledge, we didn't face any racism as a group, but each of us faced it on our own. I faced a lot of sexism and racism in my time. There was a song, "Meet me with your black drawers on", and when we'd play that song, the musicians would walk through the audience, through the aisles. It's an old musician gimmick. When we get to the chorus and say, "Meet me with your black drawers on," Reid and Nolan would say, "you got 'em on!? You got 'em on!?"* She laughed. *"The audience loved it! Reid was like the Bear and the Fox. Richard was the bear."* She laughs.

"How was your experience playing with Richard?"

"Everyone in our group new how to act. We had manners, nobody smoked Dope, and each one could teach the other. Once in a while I would get mad at someone doing the lights on stage and I would cuss. They didn't like to hear me cuss so when I did, the men would say, "Shut your mouth! Don't repeat it!" That was different because you often hear some really bad words when working in a band. We were like a family. We looked out for one another, and we were dedicated to excellence when we played our "sets." We were kind of a "spiritual" band." Jeannine recalls. *"You could tell about his spirituality and hear it in his music when he played. Ernie said a prayer before each set, and everyone participated. After each set, we received a standing ovation. God is somethin' else, ain't he? I was very hard and strict with the guys. Running a big band is hard work and I would tell 'em what to do. In a small band everything is by consent. Each of the band members were teachers and leaders in their own right. They were never "side men" and did not have that mentality. They were a sincere group of people."*

"I admired how Richard and Althea interacted with one another, and with their children. To me, they were the perfect, classic, beautiful black family in how they loved one another, and how they raised their boys."

"At 95 years young, I no longer play the piano and with the Pandemic and its lasting effect. It's not fun to travel anymore, and I don't play with just anybody. A lot of the cats have all gone on to Glory! A former drummer, Papa Jo with Count Basie told me, "Jeannie, one day you'll find that you can play with everybody,

Part II: The Music

but can't nobody play with you." She says. *"Richard could play for anyone. We have run out of road in my generation. We were on a quest for excellence, and now, a lot of musicians use all kinds of gimmicks just to get by, use dancing, a 20-piece band to sell themselves, and we could do it on our own. It makes a difference in the sound and projection of the pieces you play. This generation is visual, and they need to see how it was done. They have no idea what it is to be in a live performance where band members are making up solos as they go along. Uh-uh. None of that is rehearsed."*

"Do you have any last sentiments you'd like to share?"

"I was blessed to have Richard as a music mate. He and John Harris set the tone for the group. They were honest, faithful, and good musicians. They gave their best in making music at all times. We never sued people who used our music. It was a tribute for us and to us. Richard is just a great human being. He and his wife are a monument to black families. I don't know what the secret was, but they had it." Jeannie said. *"Others recognize excellence when they see it."*

Kevin Eubanks, World Class Acoustic Guitar Player Close Friend of the Family

"How did you meet Richard Reid?"

"I met Richard through a man named James Williams, a great jazz piano player. We were on the East coast, in New York, and James put a group together with Billy Higgins, Bill Pierce, Richard and me. We came to the East coast after we did a record in New York. I met the entire Reid family as well. Darius and Damion were small kids. Darius often jumped off the couch and on to my back, and Damion was running around the house." Kevin recalls. "The nickname "Roughhouse Reid" had been passed on to his sons." Kevin laughs. "This had to be in the mid 80's. I remember rehearsing with Richard and his family, and I'd heard Richard on recordings, but the first time we'd played together was with James Williams. We continued to play in clubs up and down the West coast. We had a nice vibe, and we'd talk about everything when we worked together. We'd all travel in Richard's green van." Kevin laughed.

"We became best buddies, friends, but he feels more like family. Besides playing together, I was able to get close with Damion and Darius as well. Richard and Althea remind me a lot of my parents. My dad fought in the Army and was a boxer, and Richard was in the Marines and was a boxer. My mother taught music in school and churches as the music director in Philadelphia so when I met The Reid's and got to know them, it felt like home." Kevin shares. "I told my parents, they have to meet Richard and Althea. They were glad knowing I had a second set of parents on the West coast."

"Musically, we always had a great time playing together. Richard had a strong sound and groove, ya know? We had a natural way of playing together. I met a lot of people through him. Something that sticks out to me is we share the same birthday, November fifteenth. . Before I moved to California, Richard would tell me to come out so we could celebrate together. One of the church ladies would cook food for Richard, and then I would be added to the mix. Richard always got what he wanted for dinner."

Part II: The Music

Kevin says. *"One year, I asked the church lady for fried fish, just for me because the others wanted fried chicken. Richard and other musicians walked up to me and asked, "Where'd you get that fish?" I'd tell them this is my fish. Y'all get the other stuff over there. Then, Althea would walk up and take a piece from my plate, bite it, and ask, "What did you say?" Of course, I had to share with her, right."* Kevin laughs. *"I always looked forward to celebrating with him. Once I moved to California, we did it more often. Again, this is another way I felt at home with them. This also made the music better. Damion is a great drummer, and Darius and I talked throughout the year as well about a lot of things. We were intentional about staying in touch."*

"How would you describe Richard as a father?"

"If I had to describe Richard as a father to his boys, I would say he's very direct. What I can really say is, if you need to take care of business just do it. Don't go around it, go through it. There are some things you have to go through. This is the feeling I got from him. They're the type of family who gets things done. If they want something, they go get it." Kevin says.

"I remember a time Richard and I were taking a plane to get to a gig and I had my guitar in the overhead space. Someone wanted to move my guitar to put their suitcase inside. Richard told the person, "Don't touch that guitar!" The person said, "Well, I gotta put my stuff away." Richard replied sternly, "Not up there you not! You need to leave it alone! Leave it alone! Don't touch it!" *"That person moved on to another space. When other passengers would reach that same space and attempt to move my guitar, other passengers who witnessed the previous exchange would say,* "Don't touch it!!!" *"They knew Richard was serious. He was very protective of the people close to him, his family, and about our instruments. I feel like he grew up that way and modeled it in his neighborhood."* Kevin says.

"What do you have to say about his handshakes?"

"I only had to shake Richard's hand one time. After that, I was done! I didn't shake his hand ever again. I watched him do that with other people and I would laugh." Kevin laughed. *"Another thing that is distinctive about Richard is when he'd play, he makes a growl. His growl is done underneath whatever he*

plays. The notes have his personality, very intense, and I believe it's a protective factor. When he plays it, he means it." Richard would say, "You know what sucka", enter a growl, and this goes on throughout the songs he plays. It's all the same. Once you know his personality, you know his growl comes out of the bass. He's not going around it, he's going through it. The growl is more than a sound. It's him, putting himself into it, his feelings which are intentional. It gives a lot of security to the rhythm section and helps them feel good, and it makes it feel more like a band all the time."

"Are there other memories you would like to share regarding Richard?"

"I'd like people to know that once Richard feels you are part of it, and he's part of it, you can count on him. I can always count on him! Music is a symbol of it, but it came before the music. It's part of his personality. Once he is dedicated to something, it shines through. Whether it's the Buffalo Soldiers or whatever, it's solid. It comes out in his family, his friendships, and his music. You can count on him!"

"Another memory I'd like to share is I once had an issue at my house with my faucet. I went back and forth to the store trying to get the right part. Richard called me and asked, "Whatchu doin'?" "I told him my faucet was broken." Richard said, "Aww sucka. I'm comin' out there!" "And he did! He went to the hardware store to get the stuff we needed, and when we got back, he got under the sink. I asked him to show me what he's doing for next time, and Richard replies, "Git on down here and look!" "It had nothing to do with me. And he's the same way if we are working on a record or other music, he's the same. It never felt like I owed him anything. It's what we do."

"Richard is also into cars. One day when he was at my house, he wanted to get someone to detail my car. I just happen to have a cool car. All I wanted was for it to go and stop!" Kevin laughs.

"Richard says, "I'm gonna get someone to detail your cahr. Bring it up here." "When I finally get there Richard says, "You ain't got no miles on this thing."

"No. I work during the week and on weekends I'm chillin." Kevin tells him.

Part II: The Music

"Richard said my car was going to dry up if I don't put any miles on it. He goes on to say, "I tell you what, when you ain't got nothin to do on the weekend, drive up to a place called Cambria, and call this number when you get there, Red Holloway. You don't know him so git in the cahr and go."

"One weekend, I didn't have anything to do, so I drove to Cambria like he told me. I walked around this little town for a while, and then I finally called Red. Red tells me to come over. When I arrived, Red asked, "What made you come up here?" I told him Richard made me come up, and Red burst out in laughter because he knows his friend, Richard. He and I became friends immediately. Red would call me up to take a drive to the grocery store to pick up things, or just to take a drive and do nothing. He and Richard sound alike in how they say things. He'd tell me to get him a 12-pack of Cold Cola. If it wasn't for Richard telling me to go, I wouldn't have the friend in Red that I did. I met a lot more good men because of both Red and Richard."

"Richard's work ethic is unmatched. He likes to rehearse and learn the music. We have that in common. He'll practice repeatedly. A lot of musicians just wanna play and get paid, but don't want to rehearse. The rehearsals are more intimate than the actual shows. Whenever I got a chance to work with Richard, Bill Pearce, and James Williams, we got close. Many of our rehearsals took place at Richard's house. All the fellowship and bonding go into our music. I feel like whatever we're doing, it goes into the music. Whether we're eating, talking, or joking around, all of it makes the feeling right, and our sound right." Kevin says. "Everything was more like a family vibe regardless of what we were doing. That brought a lot of us together, and we stayed together for quite a while. We weren't just there for the music. I remember doing a record with my uncle, Ray Bryant, and I didn't know Richard was into his music. Richard said in his grunting fashion, "Man, why didn't you tell me that was your uncle?" We had a great time through the entire record. As I said, once you become part of that vibe, it's a good feeling, and it's not just about the music, and the jazz community comes from that vibe. It felt more like home."

"I was once told that everyone had to stick together back in the day because "we" couldn't play in certain clubs nor stay in certain hotels. So, Friday fish fry's were necessary because we needed the camaraderie. We no longer live in those neighborhoods, and the music has changed. We get together now to do a few rehearsals, and then do a show. Back then we knew the families, members of the band, whose wife could cook, whose couldn't, and that gave us a sense of home. That comes with a certain generation." Kevin states. "When I played with certain musicians, it made me feel different about my music. I'm glad and fortunate to have come up where I got to play with musicians like Richard, older and more experienced than I, and I got a sense of family about it. Billy Higgins cracked everyone up, and those were formative years for me, and I am still close friends with all of them."

"Musicians now, want to get on a plane and not get in the hot, uncomfortable van where the true bonding takes place. The old cats would call me, tell me to look something up from history, and then call them back to share what I found. We'd talk about it and build on that. Most of it had nothing to do with music. There's something else about riding in the van. You start to know one another, their personalities, the funny one, the one that eats too much, and the one who puts too much cologne on his coat." Kevin laughs. "The one that didn't get a chance to shower sprays too much on them not realizing we gotta be in the van for a long time with him. But these are things you learn about one another. Being part of this group allowed me to have those "manly" conversations about life, or whatever."

"There's a point when one of the guys say, "I'm taking care of dinner tonight", and somebody ends up ordering two entrees. This person orders two because he wants try something different, but now it messes up the order for the next guy because he's not gonna get to order what he wants. Once you get to know these things, it creates a new conversation within the group, and each of us spoke honestly, but also kind to the other. I left with friends, not just a musician that you didn't see for another six months, or if ever again. This was a good period for me to grow up in and have a connection with people like that." Kevin remembers fondly.

Part II: The Music

"*Richard is just Richard. Don't beat around the bush. If you have something to say to him, just say it. He's an honest man. He once told me he'd blindfold me and teach me how to take a gun apart and put it back together again so I could defend myself in the dark if necessary. He said, "If you have a weapon and someone breaks into your home, you can't turn the light on to see who it is. They'll kill you!"* Kevin laughs. *"Richard said, "We learned that in the Marines." Anything I need to say to him as a lasting word would be said to him in a happier tone as his friend and as part of his family. I would ask, "When's the party?" And then I would ask the church lady to fry me some fish."*

Nolan Shaheed, World Class Trumpet Player – Family Friend

"WHAT WAS YOUR IMPRESSION OF RICHARD when you first met him?"

"I was impressed by Reid from the first time I met him." Nolan says. *"I've always called him Reid, rarely Richard. We played together for many years prior to me playing with him in the Christmas Cantata's at his church. We played with Jeannie Cheatham, and The Jenny and Jimmy's Sweet Baby Blues Band as well as The Tony Inzalaco Band. He was a strong bass player, and he had a strong handshake as well."* Nolan laughs. *"He'd squeeze my hand until I said, "Ouch", and then try to challenge me to an arm-wrestling contest. There was also a cat named Jeff Clayton that we played with. Richard had a beautiful tone and a nice sound when we played together for recordings or regular gigs. He was nice to have around if you wanted to intimidate other people because of his grand, African American features. Richard is also a highly animated character. His facial expressions, grunts, and bold comments made it interesting and entertaining especially if the guys didn't practice or were late. He told you straight up how he felt."*

"What was it like being on the road with him, and how would you speak to his character?"

"After our gigs, he'd go straight to his hotel room. He never hung out with the guys afterwards. He's a wise man as well. I can honestly say he's the husband of one wife. He didn't have a wandering eye. Althea is perfect for him because she's a strong woman too. He needed a strong woman because he is a strong man. He always found time to be with his boys. He has a strong hand and a soft heart." Nolan explains. *"Reid and I are serious musicians, and what we do is sacred. We don't take our gift lightly, but Hollywood doesn't always depict that. You see things in the movies about African Americans as musicians, and it wasn't true about me, Richard, and the other guys who were in our core group. I don't have enough words to tell you how much I respect Reid."*

"Any other memory you'd like to share?"

Part II: The Music

"*I remember one year when we played in the Christmas Cantata with him, and I came in about 30 minutes late, as usual. This time, it couldn't be helped, but both Althea and Richard are strict about being on time. Althea was standing in the choir stand directing and she turned to watch me walk in. She stopped the choir from singing but she allowed the band to continue playing while I set up. She turned to me and gave me "the look", but Richard gave me "a sound", a strong sound from his bass. I knew not to look in his direction.*" Nolan laughs. "*When that song was finished, Althea turned to me and said aloud, "Welcome Nolan. Everyone welcome Nolan to rehearsal!" The choir did just that and then laughed at her doing. Althea told me what song and page we were on, and we continued, but you best believe I heard it from Reid when rehearsal was over. Yea, he's a genuinely good guy that Reid. Very humble*". Nolan laughed."

George Bohanon, World Class Slide Trombone Player Family Friend

"TELL ME ABOUT YOUR RELATIONSHIP WITH RICHARD REID?"

"I've known Richard Reid for more than 30 years now. I consider Richard a "giant of a man, spiritual and an exceptional musician." George said with pride. *"His style was versatile. Lovingly, we called him Brutus because he had a big, strong look about him, yet he we as a gentle giant. I remember we were recording a song, and some of the other musicians thought we should do it one more time. Richard said, "Ain't gon git no better than that" because he didn't want to do another take. That was that!"* George said. *"Richard had an unexpected sound when he played. He was a leader, and his philosophy was simple, "Git it right, and git it right away!" We laughed when he'd say odd things like that, but we knew he was serious."*

"There were other times we joked with him, especially about his Boston accent." Laughing before speaking, George said, *"We'd tease him and say, we can't understand you!"* Richard would say, *"go pahk the cahh"* which meant, go park the car. Richard would come back to us and ask, *"You wanna start somethin' wit me sucka?" "He's a funny guy with a great sense of humor. Again, he didn't like lazy musicians. Those who arrived at the gigs late or didn't have the correct attire bothered him. Richard was rock steady."*

While George reflects, he has a somber thought about the musicians who have passed on.

"I remember Billy Higgins worked with men who demanded quality, professionalism, and perfection. Richard likes to take care of business. He didn't play around when it came to music, rehearsals, and gigs. If you didn't know your music when you got to rehearsal, you would hear about it. His playing is clean cut, and he's an honest man. Me and his wife, Althea, are from the same area. We were practically neighbors, but we never crossed paths."

"Richard had a phenomenal career in music, but he was committed to God, and his family. We had a spiritual connection. Richard is very special. He's like a big brother even though I am

Part II: The Music

older; a brother from another mother we'd say." George laughs. *"Richard would mumble under his breath about who's the oldest between the two of us, but we all know"*, George winks. *"Richard had this grunt. It was his way of telling you what to do, not ask. He "voluntells" you what to do. Richard will say,* "You can work it out. You can work it out." *"And, of course, I do. He knows I will rearrange my schedule for him and Althea."* George assures me. *"We discussed going to him homeland, to the islands, but nothing came of it. At times, we'd discuss "Us" politics and how sick of it we were. Richard and I stay on the phone talking about this and that, and nothing altogether. His bark is worse than his bite. He's a nice man with principles. Oftentimes, when we'd play, we'd feed off of one another."* He says fondly. *"There was a time when Richard wouldn't speak up, and then one day he said,* "I've been tolerating you for a lot of years." *He called me a Sucka, we laughed, and it's been great ever since. Like I said, he's a special individual."*

John B. Nickens, III, Musician - Family Friend

IT IS 4 O'CLOCK AM DURING THIS INTERVIEW VIA ZOOM.

"Good morning. How did you become acquainted with Richard and Althea?"

"*Richard, Althea, and I became acquainted in 1986 or so when I began playing at St. Stephen. I came on as a replacement for a former musician. Once I got to the church and people noticed who I was, Althea grabbed me and asked me to play for the Chancel choir. Subsequently, I met Richard then. We had a connection we never knew of.*" John remembers. "*As a child, I played piano, organ, and saxophone. I took piano and saxophone lessons for a long time. I was in single digits, the third grade at eight years old. My first saxophone teacher worked at Grant Music Center in Midtown Shopping Center which no longer exists, but it is a beacon of light for jazz artists. My teacher was Charles Owens. Years later, I found out we had mutual acquaintances because of that school. I learned his colorful personality, and I know him well.*"

"Can you tell me more about your relationship with Richard?"

"*Through many rehearsals in confines of his garage which was converted into a practice studio, we had wonderful times and some intense times. There were several occasions where he tried to impede my musical skills by shaking my hand. I used to wear rings on my hand, and I learned that if I get my hand in his palm correctly, my hand would not suffer. I called him the "hand crusher."* John says while laughing. "*The handshake is who he is. He has a gruff exterior and personality, but he is such the opposite, but you have to know him on that level to understand that. He is a tender teddy bear. The gruffness, the handshakes, and the tough rehearsals, those are during labors of love when you're birthing the music. He also reminds you of what you're not doing. That's part of who he is, and I love him for that.*"

"*When I met him, he was playing the standard, electric bass. I didn't see the upright until I got involved in the Cantata. I knew what I was in for because of having the same associations and I knew he would be quite proficient in playing. There was a time we went to Glorieta, New Mexico to minister in music, and we had a*

Part II: The Music

great time. We were in a thunderstorm and the choir was singing. As we played and sang the Spirit of God was in that place and there was a clap of thunder! Althea and I affectionately refer to that song now as "The Thunder Song." It's been more than 40 years, and we still call it that." John says.

"What else can you tell us about Richard's personality?"

"Richard has been around a long time, telling me what to do, and because of his gruff personality and needling you, you may feel that he has disdain for you, but it's the opposite. If he is bothering you and says what you're not doing, then you know you're okay in his book. If there's a situation when he does not prefer your presence as a priority, he is silent. It's hilarious, and quite something to experience! I learned this early on from Althea. I really love this guy." John says. *"To know him is to love him. I've had many wonderful experiences and memories with him that are rich. When my wife and I were dating, Richard was playing at the Suppler Club in the mid 90's. Richard was playing in a quartet, and we felt so special because we knew one of the band members."*

"It is hard to pin down the many conversations and words of wisdom shared over the years. No nuggets of wisdom, but I remember when Darius was small, and when I would visit the Reid's home, Darius would lower his head and run into my stomach. I couldn't discipline him, so I avoided going over to the house." John laughs).

"Richard continuously counted during practices. It was very interesting." John says. *"We've had quite a few sayings. When we were ministering at another church in Covina, Althea, Richard, and I used the word nucleus. This isn't meant to be funny, but we all understood what it meant. If Richard thought he could scare anyone, I would call Althea and she would straighten him out. She is my kryptonite for him."* John laughs.

"The character traits that I remember from being associated with them are when I initially met them, I was in my early 20's, I had only played for one church. I wasn't challenged to read music because the church I played for had me play by ear. But with Richard, I developed the character trait to practice because more than a few times, Richard would get under my skin intentionally. I decided that I never wanted to hear his mouth, so I made sure I

practiced to keep his "chatter" down. He motivated me to practice more because I didn't wanna hear it. Even if you practiced profusely, Richard still made comments under his breath." John recalls.

"Can you share any family-related memories with us?"

"I've ridden in the green van. Richard had his upright bass case painted the same color to match the van. Another thing is, you can't go visit him and stay too long because he would make you go on errands with him whether you wanted to or not. We would go to the bank, the store, or wherever he wanted to go. He'll talk to you whether you listen or not as well. His Boston accent made things funny. I would ask him to say "dark", and he would say "dock." I would laugh and he never knew why." John says. *"Another fun fact is, Richard has dual citizenship. He is Bajan in descent and he also Bostonian. Bajan means he's from Barbados. Many of the men I met early on as a young man, I ended up playing with them in Cantata's. The invited musicians also played with Charles Owens, an American jazz saxophonist. That was a wonderful connection."*

"I broke bread with them many times, and Althea is a wonderful chef. I'd play the piano as well. It was like rehearsal with food. Great times!" John says. *"They've been to our home as well and my wife cooked for them over holidays and other important events. It's always the same. Richard doesn't change. You don't have to wonder which Richard you will get. He's a wonderful, wonderful character. Another funny memory is musicians fearing that they would be hit over the head with his satchel of gold coins. We teased him for years about that."*

"Richard is a generous man, thoughtful of others. I remember Richard went to Tokyo in 1991, and jokingly, I asked him to bring me something back. He brought me a Japanese robe. I was very grateful for that because he remembered me" John says. *"It's a treat knowing you can't take him at "face" value. I used to be afraid of him when I was in my 20's, but now, he doesn't scare me anymore. It is entertaining to see those who don't know that about him. I love having that inside track. With Richard, it's not moods, they co-exist and it's never a dull moment. You will never be bored around him. He's told me of how he met Althea, and his*

Part II: The Music

relationship with her mother. The times we shared with both sides of the family has brought me joy. You don't know the joy until you reflect because at the time of the discipline it didn't feel like joy."

"Are there any last words you would like to share?"

"As a lasting tribute I want to say, thank you for being you, Richard. One of the things people don't get to see is Richard is a believer. You should ask him to pray. He's solid about his belief and what he believes in. Working in close confines afforded me that opportunity. He doesn't search for words. He knows what he wants to say." John assures. *"Back in the day, if Richard is in a hurry he glides and strolls. He doesn't rush. I've never even seen him trot. He is a smooth brotha. Darius gets that from him and is considered "little Richard" not to be confused with Little Richard."* He laughs.

"In all his gruffness he has inspired me, and it's been a wonderful ride. I have over 36 years of playing music with him, and it has been great. There was a time when I would see pictures of all these Jazz Cats on the wall, and when I called off their names, Richard knew every one of them. I love him and all of the Reid's. Richard, Richard, Richard! I can't wait to see him so I can needle him and show him how much I love him because he loved me."

Carl Neder — Local Business Owner - Friend

"How and when did you meet Richard Reid?"

"*Richard and I met at Tucker Tires in 1983-1984. I've known him almost as long as I've known my wife.*" Carl laughs. "*When I started working there, he was a regular customer. We hit it off from the beginning. We talked about music and things like that. From that point on, whenever he needed tires, or just wanted to talk, he would call me, and I'd tell him to come on over and we would chat for hours. When he came in, everyone knew him. We enjoyed one another's company. He has quite the personality. He comes for one thing initially, then returns because he's built a rapport.*"

"*When I first met him, he drove a horribly beat up, green-colored Dodge van. He put his bass and other instruments in there and drove them around for gigs. Eventually, I put some custom tires on it to make it look better, and sometimes it needed body and paint work. A 10-minute visit easily turned into two hours.*" Carl remembers. "*Food was also a topic we shared. Once in a while, we would have a chili cook-off at the office, and we'd call him over to come sample some of the food. The more he came in, the more he got involved with the other guys in the shop. We talked about places we'd like to travel, or restaurants where we could get a good pastrami sandwich. There were times when he would bring Althea, but not too often. This was his place to hang out.*" Carl laughs. "*As his sons grew up, they attended the same school as my boys, so that was something we had that in common as well. The two main things we shared were music and food, and it got more interesting as time moved on.*"

"Have you done his famous handshake?"

"*At Tucker Tires, initially, we didn't do the famous handshake that everyone talks about. We slugged one another on the shoulder for about 10 years. We were young and stupid then. Reid would catch the guys off guard, and left many men bruised. After those 10 years, he began shaking hands, and he would crush these guys. It was just best to keep your hands in your pockets when we were in his presence.*" Carl says.

"*Richard often shared about the gigs he played, and the cruises he went on. Our fun times were more general than specific.*

Part II: The Music

We didn't discuss artists, but I knew he played jazz. He brought two of his CD's to the shop and we played them often. He was quite a celebrity with us. I played piano and keyboard at my church and that was also something we connected through. I wasn't on his level, but he didn't care." Carl says.

"I respected Richard Reid. In our circle at Tucker Tires, we all respected him. It was a reverent relationship, and knowing he was a classy musician who liked hanging out with us left us in awe. We were still buddies and he never treated us differently. His size didn't scare me, but he had a sharp bark. The younger guys were a little intimidated, but he is a silent giant. He'd come in and raise a ruckus sometimes. We called him, "Reid" as a nickname. We're guys so we don't make up fancy names. That's not what we do at Tucker."

"Is there anything else you'd like people to know?"

"I want to share something people may not know. Richard has a love for his boys that is incomparable. As they grew up, went to school, moved on in the music world and the other in the business world, you could tell by the look in his eyes and the way he spoke that he really loved his boys, and he was very proud of them. It was always noticeable when Richard spoke of them. When he told stories about them, he was firm and loving in the way he brought them up."

"Richard often invited us to the Easter and Christmas Cantatas at his church; to come see his wife direct, and to hear Richard play. He would say, "Don't be a sucka! Come on!" "Because our church was having a concert at the same time, I never got to attend, and that is one of my biggest regrets not being able to watch and listen and worship with him."

Debra Pettus - Family Friend

"How are you connected with Richard Reid and his family?"

"My connection and friendship with Richard Reid came through my dear sister, Althea, his wife. Althea and I taught in the same school for nine years. During that time, Althea and I would often visit our favorite haunts, or I would be invited to come over to the Reid home for dinner and a movie. I was put in charge of bringing the movies and always made sure to include action and western titles in the mix as I found those genres were Richard's favorites." Debra said. "The time that I was fortunate to have had through those weekend afternoons and evenings in the Reid home were rich. I learned so much being around both Althea and Richard. There were many interesting conversations had from the films we watched. Things about the Buffalo Soldiers, and life and its impact on the lives of others. Richard and Althea's lives are an amazing tapestry of experiences that have given them a wealth of wisdom which deeply enriched those who have been fortunate to know them as individuals and as a couple."

"What else can you tell us about his character?"

"Richard exercises the gift of sharing, whether through his musical genius, his knowledge and experiences, his home, and even on vacation. On several occasions, I was allowed to crash the Reid's week-long vacation for a night or two and hang out with them which was great fun. They are a blessing to be around." Debra says. *"Whenever Richard would share stories of his life or the lives of others, I listened intently, absorbing all that he shared. For example, he talked to me about time management which I sometimes struggled with. He said,* "If you arrive at your destination at the time on the call sheet, you are already late. You got to get to your location early enough to have the time to set up whatever equipment is necessary to carry out your task and be ready to play by the time on the call sheet." *It was simple advice couched in visuals that I grabbed, and now hold onto to this day. Thank you, Althea and Richard for bringing me into your lives and allowing me to learn and grow as a human being. I am reminded of the Bible verse,* "As iron sharpens iron, so on man sharpens

Part II: The Music

[and influences] another [through discussion]." **Proverbs 27:17, The Amplified Bible.**

Cheryl Brown - Family Friend

"Tell us about your relationship with Richard Reid?"

"First, I would like to speak about how I really got to know Richard. I was already attending the church and singing in the choir when I officially met him. My first impression was that I was afraid of him. He's a big guy!" I laugh, but Cheryl doesn't. "Althea was stern enough, so when he walked into the sanctuary, he had this thing about him where you know he's not to be messed with. One day, for 8 am service, I was living in Los Angeles, California at the time, and usually one of my choir members would check on me if I'm not there at a certain time. I had overslept and didn't make it in time. I was, however, able to make it to the 11 am service. Before the service began, I entered through the side door. Another choir member approached me after the service saying, "Girl, you got here in 20 minutes, so you could have sang with us. How fast were you driving?" They laughed. "During our conversation, Richard was listening and overheard how fast she'd gotten to the church from Los Angeles to La Puente. Richard gave me a neck choke from behind. Usually, there's no chit chat or joking between the two of them, it's usually hello and good-bye. "The whole time he was scolding me, he had me by the neck. I felt like a two-year-old." Cheryl said. Richard says, "I heard that conversation. Do you know that's suicidal? Anytime you're driving on the freeway going over 70 mph, it's suicidal." "I told him I didn't know that.", She recalls. "Richard goes on and on, and still has me by the neck. When he finally turned me loose, I told him I would slow down. I told Althea what happened, and her response was, "He only does that to the people he cares about." From that conversation on, there was more conversation between Richard and I, and I never forgot that he thought enough of me to pull me aside to talk to me; someone who I was afraid of. I felt like one of his kids. My father would pull me aside when I came in past curfew. I would rather have a whippin' than to have a lecture. The same was for Richard." Cheryl said.

"What was it like visiting them at home?"

"My first visit to the Reid's home was because of our mutual friend, Donna Turner. Donna had to stop by the house to pick-up

Part II: The Music

something, and I had to use the restroom. I asked Donna to ask them if I could come in. We entered through the back door, and Althea pointed in the direction I was to go for the restroom. As I headed in that direction, everyone in the home harmoniously said, "Oh no! Take your shoes off!" I'm wiggling trying to take off my shoes and we laughed about it." Cheryl says. *"Over the years since, sometimes I call or just show up and knock on the back door without calling if I want to be devious. They know the nut is coming!"* She laughs. *"There is a nickname given to me by one of their family members. They call me "Badness." This is because I'm always getting into something. I don't remember what I said or did at church to earn the name. From that day, the name stuck. By the time the nickname got to Richard, it was all over the church. Richard and Althea still call me by that name."*

"Can you give us a little more insight to your relationship with Althea *and* Richard?"

"Me, Althea, and Richard were more like brother and sister after some time. Once I got closer to Althea, I was able to see the other side of Richard. He does not play! He is still scary looking, but a true teddy bear. If you're not in the inner circle, you wouldn't know it."

"Something fun to know about them is, there was a time when Althea had to lock up the church, but Richard felt she was taking too long. He was rushing her, and he was antsy about going on their trip the next day. He wanted to get home. Cheryl went back into the church to let Althea know how Richard was feeling. Althea said, "he just wanna go home and take the tires off their classic vehicle and put the car on blocks." *"Sometimes, Richard would do this because a neighbor across the street had a classic vehicle similar to his and it was stolen. For a while, he did this to prevent theft. Though he had a cover on the vehicle, taking off the tires would ensure it wouldn't be stolen."*

"There was another time when Althea went to Disneyland, and a nurse was stopping by for Richard during his recovery from hip replacement surgery. Cheryl and I (Laura) shared the shift to keep an eye on Richard. Richard attempted to talk Cheryl into

buying him a hamburger." We both laughed. I joined in to share my portion of that day as well. I shared how he also convinced me to purchase six bags of jellybeans for him. Althea saw me on the cameras and called Richard about it. His eyes grew large, and he was silent." Laura says. "*Afterwards, Althea called me. She said,* "were you at the house today?" Yes, I said. "What did you give to Mr. Richard?" I responded, *"I'm sorry, but I cannot divulge that information."* Althea replied, "that's okay. I'll find out what it is." All I could do was keep my mouth closed from then on." Cheryl and I continued laughing.

Another memory Cheryl remembers is giving Richard a small, six-inch cake one night after rehearsal. She had an extra one and gave it to him. When Richard and Althea got home, and after Althea came out of the shower, she noticed Richard was chewing. Althea says, "all she saw was the crumbs, and if she hadn't come out when she did, she never would have known."

"Do you have another funny memory to share?"

"One day, my sister was in town and Richard was coming by. Richard pulled up and blew the horn for me to come out. My sister asked, "who is that blowin'?" I told her it was Richard. My sister says not to go out to him because he blew his horn. Because my sister is feisty, she goes out to the car, bends down to speak to him through the window and says, "Don't no whores live here!" Cheryl laughed. *"Richard sized her up, and they went back in forth in conversation. My sister was still in town the next time Richard came by. This time, he brought Althea with him. He pulls up and tells Althea to* "watch this." *Richard blew the horn again and my sister goes out to the car and said the same thing again. This time with her hands upon her hip. Althea didn't say anything. She was shocked!"* Cheryl says.

"Do you have any last sentiments or memories to share?"

"Richard will not allow anyone to touch his upright bass, nor his bass guitar. Before hip replacement surgery. Richard had trouble carrying his instrument. Cheryl and another choir member would assist him with his chair, his amp, and other items, but Richard would not allow anyone to carry his guitar. That was sacred! All Cheryl had to do was pretend like she would touch it, and he would be quick to catch her." Cheryl said. *"One night, after*

Part II: The Music

rehearsal, Richard allowed another musician to carry his guitar. Unbeknownst to us, Richard watched how this other young musician would handle his own guitar, and because he "passed the test" he allowed the young man to help him. I says to Richard, "you let a stranger help you?" Richard said, "you still can't touch it!" "Althea reiterated how Richard knew the young man took care of his own, and therefore, earned the right to assist him."

"In the time of my first encounter with Richard, it meant a lot to me. Richard is a caring person. He is firm! If I need advice for a car or in life, or whatever, he is there. When I moved from Los Angeles, he referred me to mechanics he knows in the area if anything went wrong with my car. I've overheard him giving advice over the years." Cheryl says. "But that neck thing...whoo chile. I once gave him a bottle of eggnog. For those who don't know, Richard loves it! He gets it every year. I used to go and purchase it for him, but one year I didn't feel like going so he came by to pick me up and made me show him where to go. It is now our annual tradition!"

Ryan Suchanek (Suh-hahn-neck) — A Friend from the Local Dodge Dealer

RYAN SUCHANEK (SUH-HAHN-NECK) works at the local Dodge dealer. It's like any other office you find in a car dealership; offices surrounded by glass offering no privacy, phones are ringing off the hook, customers and servicemen and women are passing by looking in, and tables and chairs neatly partnered in a corner. As we prepare to record, I noticed a largely framed collage of photos of professional NASCAR drivers on his office wall. When he was a kid, Ryan always liked watching this event. When his grandfather passed away, this picture was left to him on his grandfather's orders. This shows the tremendous impact that older, father-figured men have let with him and on him. Ryan pauses before he speaks about Richard as if to gather his thoughts to be reverential and honoring as he is still living. Yet, he wants to share his heart as if he is solely responsible for his lasting legacy.

"What was the camaraderie like between you and Richard Reid?"

"It is an honor to be part of this project. After giving it much thought, I understand why Richard chose me to speak. Our relationship began nearly 20 years ago. I can't remember our first meeting, but I do remember he had a sneaky handshake." Ryan said while laughing. *"Richard told me I had to learn how to shake a man's hand. Actually, I felt as if Richard tried to break my hand."* He said, "This is how a man shakes hands." *"There were a few times when I would try and zing him, and beat him to the punch of the handshake, but I was only successful once."* Ryan says. "Initially, Richard didn't discuss music with me. We only talked about cars. It wasn't until a couple years later when he was getting ready for his church, Christmas recital, a Cantata. He brought in a flyer that advertised the program. I wasn't able to go for about two years because of my busy schedule, but he kept inviting me. Then, there was a time when he brought in one of his CD's." Ryan said. "He said, "This is my record. Take a look at it." *I took it home and showed my wife. I usually don't get into much conversation with my wife about work, but I have shared the many conversations with*

Part II: The Music

her about Richard in the past. I showed her the CD he gave me. As I reflect, my wife and I were so touched that someone, a customer, would invite us to one of their events at church. My wife thought it was really cool." Ryan remembers. "Then, to have that same customer give me a copy of their album was even better. Each time Richard would come into the dealership, he would bring his car in to show me a new upgrade. He loved to show off his car. He would brag about a chrome bezel (a chrome strip he bought to put under his window) and invite me to test drive his car with him. A funny thing happened one day after he gave me the album. I went downstairs and my wife was listening to his CD while she washed dishes. She was dancing to the groove of the jazz. The next time I saw Richard, I told him of my wife's behavior and his face lit up. After this day, each time Richard came in he would ask if my wife was still listening to the CD. I would tell him yes." Ryan said. "We listened to his CD when doing chores around the house, and any other event that required music. It was always fun to see her dancing, and to see his facial expression."

"Being the Service Advisor is not an easy job. We deal with irate customers that have different personalities and expectations. If the expectation is not met, there's a different result because of it. Richard was always the sweetest guy about it. Ever since I've done this job, we've had a great business relationship. I believe it was 90% talking about anything but business, and the rest is business. He would stay much longer than planned, talking about life more than the reason he brought his car in. Eventually, I would have to say, "Well, the phones are ringing and I gotta go," but we always had this connection. Seeing him brighten my day." Ryan said.

"We would joke around a lot and got to know one another's sense of humor very well. In my opinion, he was never hard to read. He's a big dude, and he could be intimidating be sure of that, but to me he was always loving even if things didn't go right in this business. There was a time when something happened with his Dodge Magnum. He said there was hesitation in his transmission. We tested it out, and nothing was wrong." Ryan said. "I've had my car for a long time. I know my car!" Richard said. *"I got in the car with him, and we drove around for 45 minutes and there was no issue."* Richard said, "I don't know where the problem went?" *"We laughed. He never got too high on himself, or too low. Just an even keeled man. He trusted me. He trusted us to take care of his vehicle, and it was always great to see him and his sons. When we establish a relationship like this with a customer, it brings light to our day because we work hard to take care of their cars and help people."*

"Are there any last thoughts you would like to share?"

"I would like to say thank you for trusting us with your business, though that sounds impersonal, it's not. To have someone bring their vehicle to you not once, not twice, but year after year is trust." Ryan says. *"I was a young service advisor moving up in the company, and Richard gave me great insight of what the business is. It makes you feel great to help people. Oftentimes, it's just customers who come and go, but Richard comes in and never really left. It was continuous. He was no longer a customer, he was family. I've been doing this more than 15 years, and serviced thousands of vehicles, and met thousands of customers. There are probably five people who've impacted my life in a way that I felt I could be good at this. Richard is one of those people"*

"I'm not perfect, but I have a God-given gift with the small things. I am personable. He made me feel good about my work and treated me like family and made me a better Service Advisor. I'm in this seat because of men like Richard. He makes me want to be a light whenever I meet new people. I'm sure he has other favorite places where he frequents and knows the clerks by name and busts their (explicit) when he sees them just like he does me." Ryan says while laughing.

"One more thing, Richard brought in his "Scooby-Doo" van once. I'd never seen this vehicle before. He's had it for decades, and we never discussed it. That vehicle was awesome! Richard always took care of his cars. He said he brought it in because a tree branch fell on the roof of it. From that day forward, anytime he was in the van and drove by, he would stop in the dealership to show me something so small as an air freshener to ask me if I liked it. He really hooked it up. Anytime I would see a van like his when driving around I would think of Richard. He put his own little

Part II: The Music

stamp on everything! What I know of him is very small, but he is very impactful to me and my life. I am just one, but you could interview any of the people who work here, and they would have great things to say about him." Ryan says with pride. *"I had to kick him out on numerous occasions because I would have 5 customers waiting, but he didn't care. He would look around and say,* "This is my time."

Family Photo Album

Part II: The Music

Althea and Richard Reid

Left to Right: Darius on the piano, Richard Reid on Upright Bass, and Damion on drums (1992).

Part II: The Music

Top; Left to Right: Darius, Donna Turner (Auntie Donna), Damion, and Richard Reid having lunch at a local restaurant.

Bottom; Left to Right: Damion, Lewis Howard Ellis, Mary Ellen Redd, lovingly called, "Boom Boom", Althea, Darius, and Donna Turner.

The Reid Family

Darius, Althea, Richard, and Damion

Part II: The Music
In Memory of "Auntie" Donna Turner – Dear Family Friend

Donna Turner (Auntie Donna), and Melba Ellis, Althea's mother (Boom Boom).

Richard A Reid: The Man, The Music, and His Ministry

LIVING LEGEND FOUNDATION 2012

Part II: The Music

Richard Reid, Althea Reid, & Red Holloway

Steve Turre, George Bohanon, and Richard Reid at a Night Club in Los Angeles

Part II: The Music

U.S. MARINE CORPS

Cpl R.A. Reid

U.S. MARINE CORPS BOOT CAMP

Part II: The Music

Althea Reid, Richard Reid & Jeannie Cheatam

Richard A Reid: The Man, The Music, and His Ministry

Musical Tributes Continued with Dedications

Family Portrait Album by Richard Reid

1. Barbados Mir (Dedicated to Mildred I. Reid, Richard's Mother)
2. Three Four Al *(Dedicated to his wife, Althea)*
3. Dearing Dar *(Dedicated to his son, Darius)*
4. No I Mad *(Dedicated to his son, Damion)*
5. Beauty and the Beast
6. Elements Reunion
7. Seven Minds
8. Be Real Special
9. Sting Thing

Have A Cup With Richard Reid & Friends

1. Have A Cup
2. Trickertism
3. Oleo
4. Mona Lisa
5. Just Rolling Along
6. Blues for Gwen
7. Hardknocks Blues
8. When I Fall In Love

Richard A Reid: The Man, The Music, and His Ministry

Richard Reid's Legend

Education – B.M. – 1977 New England Conservatory of Music (NEC)

Artists with whom he has worked:

Singers

Aretha Franklin	Eddie "Cleanhead" Vinson
Eddie Jefferson	Joe Williams
Don & Alicia Cunningham	Helen Merrill
Ernestine Anderson	Spanky Wilson
Tavares	Marlena Shaw
Gloria Lynn	Saundra Reeves Phillips
O.C. Smith	Johnny Hartman
Solomon Burke	Jeane Carne
Randy Crawford	Percy Mayfield
Linda Hopkins	Jimmy Witherspoon
Clyde McPhatter	Ernie Andrews
Maxine Brown	Bill Henderson
Etta James	Mary Stallings

Instrumentalists:

Bobby Hutcherson	Eddie Harris
Bobby Shaw	Clark Terry
Henry Butler	George Bohanon
Milt Jackson	David "Fathead" Newman
Buddy Collette	Horace Silver
Harry "Sweets" Edison	Frank Collette

Part II: The Music

- Kenny Berrell
- Phil Wilson
- Marshall Royal
- Roy Haynes
- Kevin Eubanks
- Pharoah Sanders
- Tiny Grimes
- Richie Cole
- Slide Hampton
- Art Farmer
- Lou Donaldson
- Johnny "Hammond" Smith
- Jaki Byard
- Donald Byrd
- Patrice Rushen
- Al Cohn
- Bob Cooper
- Philly Joe Jones
- James Williams
- Freddie Hubbard
- Oscar Brashear
- Dick Whittington
- Donald Harrison
- Marvin "Smitty" Smith
- Roy Hargrove
- Buddy Montgomery
- Alan Dawson
- Bobby Bryant
- John Collins
- Sonny Stitt
- Williams "Phil" Pierce
- Hank Crawford
- Philipp Philips
- John Handy
- Terry Gibbs
- Eddie "Lockjaw" Davis
- Plas Johnson
- Monsier Santos
- Doc Cheatam
- Snooky Young
- Frank Morgan
- Harold Land
- Jeannie & Jimmy Cheatham
- Billy Higgins
- Elvin Jones
- Smith Dobson
- Red Holloway
- Benny Carter
- Steve Turre
- Ray Bryant

Richard A Reid: The Man, The Music, and His Ministry

Phil Upchurch   Jeff Clayton

Ricky Woodard

Group Memberships

*Currently a member

James Williams Quintet   Benny Carter All Stars

Donald Byrd Quintet   Harold Land Quintet

Charles Owens Quintet   Horace Silver Quintet

Sonny Stitt & Red Holloway Quintet   Freddie Hubbard Quintet

Billy Higgins Quintet   Roy Hayes Hip Ensemble

Billy Green & The Conductors   Plas Johnson Quartet

Alan Dawson Quartet   Buddy Collette Quartet

Pharoah Sanders Quartet   Red Holloway Quartet *

Eddie Harris Trio & Quartet   Kenny Burrell Trio

Harold Jones Trio   Henry Butler Trio

Jaki Byard Trio   Buddy Montgomery Trio

Jerome Richardson & Conti Candoli Quintet

J & J Cheatham & Sweet Baby Blues Band

Discography:

Shrine – Kevin Eubanks
In Soul Music

Slow Freight – Ray Bryant & Kevin Eubanks
In Soul Music

The Last Show – Etta James & Eddie "Cleanhead" Vinson
Fantasy Records

Red Holloway & Company – Red Holloway
Concord Records

Blues in the Night – Etta James & Eddie "Cleanhead" Vinson
Fantasy Records

Hittin' the Road Again – Red Holloway
Jam 014

From the Heart – Ernie Andrews
Discovery Records 05825

Blue Minor – Claude Williamson
Japan Label

Country Fiddlers – Gunther Schuller
Columbia Records

Locksmith Blues – The Red Holloway & Clark Terry Sextet
Concord Records

Blue Phase – George Bohanon
Geobo Music, Inc.

Hot Blue & Saxy – Plas Johnson
Carrell Music Co.

Blues & The Boogie Masters – Jeannie & Jimmy Cheatham
Concord Records

Gud Nuz Bluz – Jeannie & Jimmy Cheatham
Concord Records

Richard A Reid: The Man, The Music, and His Ministry

Red Holloway Quartet w/Harry "Sweets" Edison
Chiaroschurro Records

Out of Time – George Kahn
Playing Records

Personal Discography:

Family Portrait of Richard Reid
Roughhouse_Reid Prod.

Have a Cup with Richard Reid and Friends
Roughhouse_Reid Prod.

Movie Credits:

"Blues for Central Avenue"	With Ernie Andrews
"Wild at Heart"	With Nicholas Cage
"Public Eye"	With Joe Pesci
"Corinna Corinna"	With Whoopi Goldberg

Honorable Mentions

Certificate of Appreciation

This certificate is awarded to

Richard Reid

In recognition of your contributions to Jazz & Blues, The Living Legend Foundation and the Beverly Hills Hollywood NAACP are proud to honor your contributions as a Legendary Jazz & Blues Bassist. Your mastery of this profession is an exemplary inspiration for generations to come. We celebrate and honor you for keeping Jazz & Blues alive.

On this 27th day of September, 2012

Ron Hasson, President
Beverly Hills/Hollywood NAACP

Linda Morgan, Founder
Living Legend Foundation, Inc.

Richard A Reid: The Man, The Music, and His Ministry

someone to know
Jazzman built I.V. following with Pomona appearances

By Imani Tate
Staff Writer

Master jazz bassist Richard Reid of West Covina plays with his eyes closed so he "can feel the music."

"I'm having a conversation with the instrument," he said, not caring if "talking" to an inanimate object seems eccentric. "You can't have a good conversation if your mind is going other places."

James "Red" Holloway, the pioneering saxophonist who will be feted in an 80th birthday Sunday at the 29th annual Playboy Jazz Festival, picked Reid for his Sunday sideman at the Hollywood Bowl, because the bassist's "conversation" magically interplays with Holloway's horn.

"He's simply something else," Holloway said. "He's the upright man who weaves a wonderful musical tapestry on the upright."

Billy Higgins, jazz's most recorded drummer, called Reid "an amazing musician. You can't come up with enough adjectives to describe what he does. He literally makes the bass sing, swing, sway."

Inland Valley jazz folks packed the house when Reid and organist/pianist Johnny "Hammond" Smith jammed in weekly Jazz on the Hill concerts in Pomona and Reid led his own ensemble at the Shilo Hilltop Suites Hotel.

"Watching this man play was a different and wonderful experience musically and spiritually," recalled Dr. Beverly Guidry, Western University of Health Sciences vice president of student affairs. "If you didn't arrive early, you didn't get a seat when he and Johnny were in the house."

"He's like a Mack truck. He'll run over you if you don't get out of the way," said jazz singer Ernestine Anderson, describing Reid's playing.

The Boston native was initially a self-taught artist who played for fun, first on guitar and later on drums in the Ridge Technical High School band in Cambridge, Mass.

He played bass lines on four of his guitar's six strings in a jazz band while serving in the Marines. He'd always "liked the sound, the depth, the bottom" of the acoustic bass, so it didn't take much to pick it up for the Marine combo.

He worked as a mechanic and machinist after discharge, but played weekend Boston club dates with drummer Alan Dawson, pianist James Williams and tenor saxophonist Bill Pierce. Dawson, a first-call musician, frequently engaged Reid for gigs with notable vibraphonist Milt Jackson, singer Joe Williams, trumpeters Clark Terry and Art Farmer and saxophonists Eddie "Lockjaw" Davis and Sonny Stitt.

Pianist Rollins Griffith advised Reid to take his natural talent, get formal training and occupy the musical space where he really belonged. To assure the full-time shift, Griffith introduced him to Gunther Schuller, president of New England Conservatory of Music. Reid won

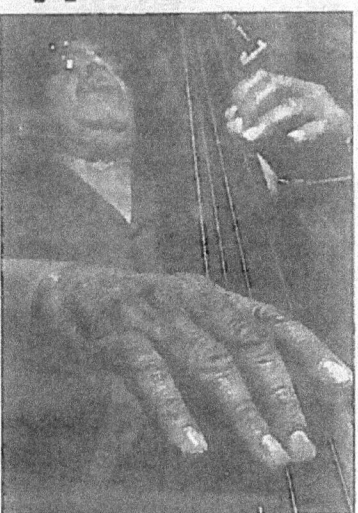

Thomas R. Cordova/Staff Photographer
The hands of master jazz bassist Richard Reid rehearse swinging rhythms to prepare for gig with pioneering saxophonist James "Red" Holloway at the Sunday set of the 29th annual Playboy Jazz Festival.

While earning a degree in acoustic and electric bass performance, Reid met his wife, Althea, a master's in music and voice student at the conservatory. She now teaches music at West Covina Christian School. Their son, Damion, won the Thelonious Monk scholarship, a degree from The New School and a reputation as a jazz drumming young lion. Son Darius, an award-winning teen pianist, shifted to sports and earned a football scholarship to Texas Southern University.

Reid's concert cohorts have included musical greats Pharoah Sanders, Eddie Harris, Harold Land, David "Fathead" Newman, Harry "Sweets" Edison, Freddie Hubbard, Steve Turre, Elvin Jones, Bobby Hutcherson, Johnny Hartman, Ruth Brown, Linda Hopkins, Cedar <cq> Walton, Horace Silver, Jimmy and Jeannie Cheatham, Jimmy Witherspoon, Gerald Wilson, Kenny Burrell, Kevin Eubanks, Aretha Franklin, Etta James and Marlene Shaw.

A master musician for four decades now, Reid, 67, still finds jazz "challenging." He loves it because "you can improvise, play what you feel, create emotional textures and musical layers."

Reid performs in the "no regrets" mode, playing like "it's going to be my last time playing. I never want to go back and say I should have done this or that. I lay it all out at that moment."

Part II: The Music

STATE OF CALIFORNIA

SENATE

CERTIFICATE OF RECOGNITION

Richard Reid

WHEREAS Richard Reid was born November 15, 1939 in Boston, MA; and

WHEREAS He began playing the bass while he was a Marine; and

WHEREAS Richard played with Red Holloway for 31 years; and

WHEREAS He is a graduate of the New England Conservatory of Music; and

WHEREAS Richard Reid has played with most of the top Jazz artists in the business. He has worked with such singers as Aretha Franklin, Joe Williams, Johnny Hartman, Marlena Shaw to name a few; and

WHEREAS He was a member of the Eddie Harris Quartet and Trio, The Horace Silver Quintet, The Harold Land Quintet, The Red Holloway Quartet and The Jimmy and Jeannie Cheatham Baby Blues Band; and

WHEREAS The Living Legend Foundation recognizes his contributions in continuing to keep Jazz & Blues alive, for future generations; and

WHEREAS, Jazz gives a powerful voice to the African American experience and is born of a diverse society, uniting people across the divides of race, region, and national boundaries, and draws from life experience and human emotion; now, therefore, be it

RESOLVED BY SENATOR RODERICK D. WRIGHT, on this twenty-seventh day of September, 2012, that Ernie Andrews, Wally Holmes, Richard Reid, Leroy Harrison, & Piper Alvez be commended for their contributions to the world of Jazz & Blues, and extended sincere best wishes for continued success in the future.

RODERICK D. WRIGHT
MEMBER OF THE SENATE, 25TH DISTRICT
CALIFORNIA STATE LEGISLATURE

PART III, HIS MINISTRY (Allegro)
Lively, cheerful, or brisk

DURING TODAY'S INTERVIEW, IT IS JUST ALTHEA AND RICHARD. We are still in the midst of the Covid-19 pandemic, and we are semi-social distanced at the patio table in the backyard. Though it is mid-July, God is gracious in holding back the heat, and he even threw in a cool breeze once in a while to let us know He is there. A few airplanes are flying overhead as well as a flock of green parrots who, in Althea's opinion, only show up because their sons Darius and Damion are there. These things are slight distractions, but they also add to the title of this chapter of the book. Richard's wife, Althea, gives much insight to their college years, early marriage years, and other historical things that took place.

Althea was born in Detroit, Michigan. As far as she knew, she loved her world, and because Detroit was the Motor City and things were booming! They were in their own, middle class, African American community. This is because most of the adults were either working as a teacher, or in the car plants, and they were doing well at that time. It lasted just before her senior year of high school, but then the riots broke out, and the explosion, the Summer of 1967. There was the Watts riot and then the Detroit and Chicago riots. All of these were popping up around the same time. Althea had always loved music. She began with taking piano at the age of four and played that for a long time. She'd had an Italian piano teacher from the beginning until she graduated from high school. Since her parents had her using the church piano for lessons and her dad was the superintendent, she played for Sunday School and the worship services every Sunday. She was his musician.

Part III: His Ministry

She grew up in a two-parent household as an only child. There were cousins around, but not during her adolescent years. Her mother incorporated cousins from Althea's father's side because they were a larger family, Althea would have someone to interact with, and it relieved pressure from both sides having a large family, and this, in turn encouraged Althea to share. There was a time as a child when Althea would not share and if she claimed everything as hers, her mother would send her toys and anything else home with her cousins. By the time she'd gotten to junior high school and formed her own world, her cousins had moved away. The neighborhood she grew up in was deemed safe and worrying about being bullied or picked on was not a concern for her.

She attended Cass Technical High School which required her to claim a major. Pastor Dockery and Althea share a chuckle between them about this school. Pastor says she was allowed to attend Cass Tech and he wasn't. Althea states it's because she was smarter! One had to audition or take part in an entrance exam to attend. Because she was in her own world by now, she had since pulled away from her cousins because they weren't into music as she was, rehearsals before and after school as well as other commitments. It was consuming. Her parents were supportive of her passion for music though there weren't sure where it would take her. Her mother was a beautician in the home, and her father was an insurance salesman. When Althea entered junior high, her mother went back to school to become a registered nurse. They graduated together, Althea from junior high, and her mother from nursing school. This is when her mother began working full-time on the graveyard shift to ensure someone was home during the day for Althea. The rules on Althea were strict. Her mother wanted to know who the boy was, who their family was, their ancestors, etc...She had female friends, but they were all musicians. They spent time at her house, but her outings at other's homes was selective. Once her parents learned more, she was able to venture out more. Althea did not attend a lot of parties due to her busy schedule. Days or nights when there were no music rehearsals at school, she was at church. She and her family made their own traditions.

After high school graduation, she attended undergraduate school at Olivet College in Michigan for four years. They didn't mind her going away to college, but they did not want her to go too far too soon since she had just turned 16 years old. Remember, she's a smart one; double promoted in one year. Althea had a teaching job for three years while Richard was still in school. After those three years, they were married and left Massachusetts. She was the first African American teacher, and as mentioned before, they highlighted this because things were opening, and they wanted that representation of her coming from the Conservatory. There were other opportunities in Maine as well, but she did not want to be up there alone because the demographics was not favorable. She made extra money through graduate school by singing at a church that needed a soloist. This was her job each Sunday, and this boosted the choir. Through this venture, she met lifelong friends.

Note: *"The conservatory is where Coretta Scott-King attended, in the Northeast where legitimate segregation is taking place. There were those at MIT, Harvard where there are sprinklings of African Americans in the Cambridge area with colleges and universities. There was not a large group. They were selective, but they were trying to present an image, bringing in just enough color, or the cream of the crop; those who would make a good name for the college. The word "inclusive" or "affirmative action" had not been coined as of yet. By the time Althea and Richard were out of college, those aforementioned terms began in full force. There were certain professors who stood back to see what you were made of, but Althea did not experience it on campus. Richard received his Bachelor of Music, and after graduation he married Althea, and then moved to California.*

Althea met Richard's mom at his graduation recital. She must have made a good first impression on her because a lot of Mrs. Reid's recipes were given to Althea. It was known that Richard's mother did not give out her recipes to just anyone. Mrs. Iona Reid stated, "This one here that he feels heaven and earth was created just for him." Everyone laughs at the remembrance of these memories. *Thinking back to their early days of marriage, Althea mentions that Damion was born just under two years after they* were married. Richard was gone quite a bit, and one of his gigs took him away for three months. Upon his return, he reached out to Damion and was rejected. Since children change so much in the early years, he'd forgotten who Richard was. Now, when Richard traveled, he would not stay as long to preserve his relationship with his son. This was also the time Althea decided to start teaching. Damion and Althea settled into their routine and when Richard returned from traveling, he had to adjust. Althea taught in Pomona until Darius was born. She, then stayed home with Darius. Althea reflects on her boys' names and their meanings. Since Althea was an only child and no boys carried her maiden name, Ellis, and they wanted to be intentional about what they named their sons, she and Richard incorporated Althea's maiden name as well as an African name in both Damion and Darius' full names, and both of their sons' names spell out the acronym D.E.A.R.

Richard continued to work as a musician. His favorite country to play in was Germany because they appreciated music especially jazz. He dealt with segregation everywhere he went, but he remembers when they were going across territories in Germany to France, the police would harass them about their passports, and it nearly discouraged him to stop traveling, but Redd Holloway told him, *"That's just something we deal with. That's all."* Richard also played in England, but his experience was not great due to the attitudes of the British. He remembers the comedy of it all and laughs.

While walking down the street, Richard sees an orange tree and he picks one. Richard was told by a vendor that he couldn't have *that* orange. When asked why, the vendor reached down in a drawer to reveal oranges that were brown, damaged, rotten-looking, and squishy. Richard said, *"I ain't buyin that!"* The vendor said he had to, but Richard told him to keep that orange to himself and walked away. Richard often encountered confrontation in England because *others* felt privileged. Every country had their own attitudes that he had to deal with. Going out after a gig was a hassle so after he finished playing, he'd just go back to his hotel room. Certain gigs caused for a certain bass. When he played with Redd Holloway, he played the electric bass because it cost more to ship the upright bass due to it needing to be shipped in a hard case the cost was in upwards of $200. Depending on where he was going and how they'd handle his instrument was also part of deciding which bass to use.

Althea mentions they joined St. Stephen Missionary Baptist Church in October of 1978 while she was pregnant with Damion. Shortly after joining, Pastor McCall approached both of them. He found out she and Richard were musicians from another church member, and her exact words to Pastor McCall were, *"She is a musician, and you need to use her."* Pastor McCall asked Althea to start another choir, and thus, The Chancel Choir was born. While still forming the newest choir, Richard and Althea sang with the Senior Choir. The first time The Chancel Choir sang, it was early 1979. They had 15 members. Richard played the bass and Althea played the piano. The choir grew quickly from there.

Althea mentions meeting my mother, Eloise, in the Senior Choir which causes me to pause internally at the thought of them being friends. They'd have various gatherings at Althea's home. My mother and one of the other women would sing numerous songs and became close with other female pillars of the church. They'd pray and sing, laugh, cry, and eat, all while enjoying one another's company. These women threw Althea a baby shower and blessed her with numerous gifts.

"Are there any black men who spoke into your life at this time; Men who kept you on track while traveling in country or out of the county?"

Red Holloway, Alan Dawson, his brother Bobby, and another man whose name he cannot recall. This man played with he and Billy, and he was responsible for speaking with Gunther Schuller, the President of The Conservatory during their time. Richard has played with and for a lot of musicians and thinking back to the "boogey woogey" days of early musicianship he recalls the many times he was shielded from the rejection of playing in certain clubs because of his color in Boston. Jack Hahn, a white man, told Richard that he'd been asked why he has a black bass player, and Jack Hahn said, *"it's because Richard is part of the band."* Many clubs didn't want him to play, but Jack told them if they want to use his musicians, Richard comes with the package. Jack never

Part III: His Ministry

told him about the conversations until afterwards because Jack knew how Richard would react.

When Richard moved to California, he went to see Jerry Williams perform at the Parisian Room. Jerry told Redd Holloway, *"This is the cat you need to be usin'."* Red finally gave him a shot and Richard ended up working for him majority of the time. Red said Richard was like the son he never had. Althea interjects that Richard had personal relationships with a few of the musicians where they'd fellowship, and the others were just part of a working relationship.

He remembers doing a modeling segment for a cigarette commercial. He and other musicians were taking a break after a gig and went to a small restaurant to eat. The cigarette company posters were stationed on all the tables. One of his band mates recognized him and said, *"That's you on there ain't it?"* They all laughed. This is also how Pastor McCall responded when he saw it on the wall of a door of a gas station in another state. McCall mentioned that he saw Brother Reid on a poster. By now, that ad had circulated throughout the entire country.

Part III, His Ministry, Cont., (The Family Circle)

TODAY, THE ENTIRE REID FAMILY IS TOGETHER ONCE AGAIN, and I took this moment to allow Damion and Darius a chance to give their father his flowers while he could smell them. Since we began this journey, a lot of deep things have been shared.

I would like to know how the discipline your father instilled in you shines through.

Darius answers first. *My father said,* "Do as I say, not as I do." Damion is trying to process the nature of my question. Both Damion and Darius mentioned their father taught them discipline and how to be men. What it was like to grow up as a black man, the dos and don'ts at work, at home, and how this played a role because at some point something had to change before you became men.

How did that play out? I asked.

Darius mentions he didn't get into a lot of trouble because he didn't get caught. I did, however, get in trouble for talking back all the time. Damion, lovingly nicknamed the tortoise, said he didn't have time for that. He didn't want to test the waters. *"There were a lot of life lessons, not just father and son stuff. Even though the delivery seemed harsh to others, there was always something to learn in there."* Damion adds.

"When people get older, they make mistakes. If people harp on that, they miss the wisdom in it. I've always hung out with older people, and most of my friends and the musicians I play with are older than I am. I didn't make a resume with people my age. I was always the youngest in the band and on the stage. I look at things as lessons." Damion says. *"Being the oldest I felt I had to move a*

Part III: His Ministry

little more methodically and get as much as I can just in case. There are a few things that contribute to that other than vocation. It's the thought process and how to handle oneself. My temperament stayed the same." He continues. *"My father and I are in the same field and people will tell him how I am and vice-versa. I think there's always room for growth that will help me in playing this music. It's a social experience, not just black and white. There are many levels to it. A lot of the older musicians see it as well. If you think about it, my dad got started late with having kids. Most men start having kids while they're in their 20's. He was methodical with that as well. By now, many men would have two or three kids, or moved on to their next wife. With my dad it wasn't like that. One of my favorite animals is the tortoise, wise and take time to express themselves."*

"I tested and challenged everything, especially the rules." Darius says. *"Rules are man-made, and I felt just because you say something I needed to know why because rules can change. The discipline was always there, but I didn't take things for what others said. The explanation of things was not taken at face value. As I got older, I was the only one that's not in music and it was hard to relate to someone when you don't have a clue and can think outside of that. But my core principles were there."* Darius states. *"There was distance because it wasn't understood what I did. I wandered into my own world. Things were very "iron fisted" in how things were run. There wasn't much talking, and we didn't have a say to a degree. In certain situations, it was fair. He ruled!"* Darius said and Damion concurs. *"As kids get older and become men, those discussions didn't happen, but that's just the way he was. He was tough. I wouldn't say a tortoise per se, but it does have a tough, outer shell. I would refer to my dad as an alligator. He has tough skin on the outside and it cannot be penetrated, and it has a vicious bite. That is more of what I would say. As we became adults, things shifted. Dad shifted more towards my brother because of the music. He didn't understand what I did, but we shared football then, and now. What I have become is a foreign knowledge which is fair because that isn't his world. There's still a lot of the "Do as I say, not as I do" as well."* The family laughs. *"That's just who he is."*

"What do both of you want people to know? What sense do you want your father to leave, or people to have of your father when they read this book? How do you want them to feel when he walks into a room? Darius answers first:

"My father is a bonafied king. He did it! He always owned up to his responsibilities as a Reid. These are the values he instilled in us. Everywhere he went, he was a presence, a force. He was always the biggest man in the room, not size wise, but just by who he was and is. He didn't have any softness in him. If he did, it was behind closed doors." Darius says proudly.

Damion interjects with laughter and says, *"I'm laughing because we've been joking with my dad the whole year about this very thing."* Damion goes on to say, *"he'd like people to know my father did it his way. He learned a lot, and he learned it his way. He stood for things that a lot of people are afraid to stand for, honor, respect, and culture."*

"He had a lot of integrity as well." Darius says. *"He took risks for the community. Communal effort was something he did before we were born. He's done it through the church as well. He was a servant to the cause."*

When directed to Mr. Richard, he's too emotional to respond without tears.

"I'm at a loss for words." Richard says. *"I didn't know my boys felt that way about me."* Darius mentions this is the one time he wants to be soft and it's okay.

"We can count on one hand how many times we've seen our father cry." Darius says. Althea confirms this. *"He cried at his wedding to Althea, at Althea's mother's funeral, during his 70th birthday party, and now."*

They all share a precious moment and laugh together. I also have tears in my eyes. Althea hands each of us a tissue.

Darius states, *"the best animal to compare my father to is the Grizzly Bear. When he's by himself, in his element, he wants to be left alone. If you bother bears, they roar and take your head off. That's literally how he was and is. I got a chance to see a live Grizzly Bear while growing up, and I said, that's my dad, playful and sit there alone. They don't need a lot, just the simple things.*

Part III: His Ministry

He's a man's man, but if you make him roar, that's it!" Darius warns.

"*My mother also called Richard a bear as well."* Althea adds.

"*My dad stood up for others that were weaker when right was right and wrong was wrong, and he's jump in anybody's face over it."* Darius says.

Damion makes a correction for the record in that he was not describing his father as a tortoise, but Althea says he was. Richard moves a little slower now than he used to. *"It's more of an eastern lesson. The lessons of taking your time and being aware to preserve yourself, the turtle is my favorite animal."* Damion says.

This broke up the conversation in a loving way.

"*I knew what they'd be faced with in this world. I went into the Marine Corps because I didn't see him my brother Bobby much. I was set up to attend Howard University, but I joined the Marine Corps."* Richard says.

"Rebellion!" Althea adds.

"*I ended up on the same base as Bobby. When my brother saw me, he asked me why I was here. I told him, "This is the only way I could see you."* The reception he received looked differently, and he had his own reasons for doing what he did.

"*The years spent in the Marine Corps allowed me to see how racist this country was. I said my kids would be able to take care of themselves wherever they go. I experienced a lot of racism in North Carolina, and I needed my kids to be prepared so I put them in karate when they were little. I was thrown out of a drug store because I sat down in the store to drink a Coke in North Carolina. They called the cops on me. I was wearing my Marine uniform, and I thought to myself, "Who am I wearing this uniform to protect? These white folk or my folk? Therefore, I didn't reenlist, but Bobby did. He served 26 years in the Marines. This was not for me."* Richard said. *"I dealt with it in Boston as well. When it was time to reenlist, the Colonel came to me. I was his driver, and a lot of the guys would sniff around me asking where the Colonel was headed daily. I wouldn't tell them anything. I took care of his cahr and it helped me get another stripe. When we went into town as servicemen, things were different. Even now, we still gotta deal *with the jive." He continues.* Boom Boom always stressed for the kids to read, and if they didn't know they'll find out.

As the open discussion continues, Althea spoke about the pros and cons, about how the consistency of the discipline was necessary, and it molded them to understand it was important. *"The lessons were good, and sometimes the message could be strained, but they were there. It was good to have the balance of the two to diffuse some things. There were never any lessons that Richard wanted to get across that were not good, and sometimes they had to be modified in how they were delivered."* She laughs. *"The purpose was vital because of the world we live in, and I think it paid off to help them become the men they are. The knowing, the stick-to-itiveness, the realism in the world, all of those things were taught. It was necessary so they're not walking through life blindly or at a disadvantage. The Baby Boomer generation made a mistake with the trauma they went through by sheltering their children from the truth, and they didn't want to discuss it, and I believe this put their children at a disadvantage. And you can't really know where you're going if you don't know where you came from. You don't know how to get there, or you get there on a façade."* Althea continues. *"This may be why we have so many issues even now. They were put into situations that made them believe they were not who they really were, but the world will let you know who you really are. Those things were effective for both our sons, and they had the realism of who they were. Richard was going to get out there to make sure they knew and this provided balance. Even though they attended a private school and lived in suburbia, they have to work harder."* She insists. *"You can't see your way through, and you have to be better just to be recognized. These are basic principles my parents taught me, and the ball was dropped with my generation because of the reality of what we went through. We wanted to protect our children, but it harmed them. When Damion and Darius got into the real world, they were prepared because they weren't given rose-colored picture of what life was like."*

I shared a moment with The Reid's by telling them I have benefitted from their teachings in many areas. I've known them since I was ten years old, and then and now, I fear them to a degree.

Part III: His Ministry

"But I'm the nice one." Althea says and then laughs.

"It depends on who you ask." I say with a laugh. "I know I can come to either of you if I need to especially when I need help. The things I've learned while doing this interview, I try to apply to my life. I get the references of the bear, alligator, and the tortoise. Each of them has poured into me and that is a great thing. Thank you."

"My sister, Cynthia, was a pistol." Richard adds as a random memory. *"She's very brilliant and she graduated Cum Laude. When she'd come home, she couldn't get a decent job. They had her working the counter at Woolworth's. She's on top of a lot of stuff and she has a temper. Growing up in our neighborhood, there were only three black families in the area and I had to fight my way home from grade school. I had to walk by an Irish family named The Walsh's. If anyone was outside, I had to fight. My brother Cecil seemed to carry the family on his back."*

Darius closes out with saying that his father was a man of action.

"There wasn't a lot of conversation, but he did a lot. Whenever he went away, he came back with gifts. He didn't teach us how to romance a woman, but when he came back, he always had something for mom. She had a lot of sets of knives." They laughed.

"We had to watch him to learn and figure it out. He led by example that's for sure." Damion says.

THE FOURTH MOVEMENT (ROLLICKING)
Dancing with Joy with Friends and Family
"Richard's Birthday Jam Session"

AS WE HAVE LEARNED TO NAVIGATE through the Covid-19 pandemic, we have not forgotten to celebrate birthdays. Richard and Kevin Eubanks share the same birthday, so it was only fitting they celebrate with one another and invite a couple more friends along. It is Sunday morning, November 15, 2021. Invitees to the Zoom call are Richard Reid, Kevin Eubanks, Nolan Shaheed, and George Bohanon. It is evident that each are glad to see one another as they joke about life changes such as hair loss, the changing of their hair color, and of course more music gigs. Kevin is the first to join the call from his studio, and he and Richard discuss upcoming events on television. Richard uses phrases like, "No jive, Is that so", and Kevin being a seasoned musician who has been groomed by men with an old soul reciprocates his lingo.

Joining the world in-person is part of the plan for Kevin, while Richard is enjoying his partial retirement. Though age has been kind to each of them, they seriously joke about having to take more time to warm up versus what they used to be able to do with picking up their instruments, strumming or plucking, or blowing a few notes and moving forward while working a full-time gig.

Richard's laugh clearly expresses how glad he is to see his friends. Kevin jokes about why they aren't in worship services since it's a Sunday. And if Althea isn't running the church, who is there. Althea reminds Kevin that the church is closed, and the only service available in-person is the 8 am service. Kevin shutters at the thought of being awake so early. This conversation cannot be complete without discussing being vaccinated and remembering how they survived as kids, eating at friend's homes, and drinking out of the water hose. Both men discuss how so many still do not believe in the Covid-19 vaccination.

Nolan Shaheed joins the call and the first words out of Richard's mouth to him is, "Cat Daddy!"

"Nolan, you look healthy man!" Kevin says. *Even with your gray hair."*

"You're supposed to be the youngest in the group." Richard reminds Nolan.

"I'm cold everywhere I go because my hair is gone." Kevin states. *"I may have to start wearing a wig on airplanes."* Kevin jokes!

Each of them laughs because they can relate.

"Man, I'm so blessed. I am doing well." Nolan tells them.

They all agree about how blessed they are to still be able to see one another. Age has no barriers, and the puns continue to fly about their health, their living will and trusts, and of course, dying, but they are serious-minded about the subject and expect their families to throw a party in their honor. Listening to these dear friends share old memories and future plans is heart-warming. Nolan serenades both Kevin and Richard and plays "Happy Birthday" on his trumpet.

Kevin reminds the group how they all used to celebrate back in the day. The others wanted chicken, but Kevin wanted fish. Kevin bragged how the cook at the church "hooked him up" and the other men complained. Kevin was stingy back then and wouldn't share. *"I don't even eat fish anymore."* Kevin says. I'm vegan. Both Nolan and Richard are shocked. The men are thoughtful towards one another as they discuss eating cool things they used to eat like cheeseburgers, eating fresh fruit off fruit trees, eating foods with soy, and vegetables. While listening to them talk about such things, I feel as if I need to call a doctor. I'm wondering, *"Is this what the older folks talk about?"* As they discuss testosterone levels, medical doctors, and exams, Kevin calls me out because he notices that I am laughing at hearing their conversation. They exchange names of local physicians that can "educate" them in their ventures.

George joins the call, and while he is waiting his image appears in the box sooner than he expected. He is patting the top of his hair so he'll look good when he sees his friends. George is startled by Richard's voice.

"Hey! Lookie here!" Richard yells. "It's about time you joined us."

"Have you ever heard of "Just for Me" for men?" Nolan asks.

Each of them laughs as they jab at their friend. George doesn't pay them any attention. They discuss old friends, old gigs, marriage, and digital music. During the interview, I had an expectation to hear all the juicy stuff about their gigs in the past, but I am being educated about life. As a woman, I have never been privy to these type of conversations with men, but I must say it is both informative and entertaining. I have often heard that men are babies about going to the doctor, but not these men. They "want" to take care of themselves. Kevin updates the group on a mutual friend whose health has been challenged recently, and how this doctor was able to nurse him back to good health. Nolan shares how he's experienced good doctors because they work on the whole man instead of how the Western style medicine differs from Eastern style.

As they continue this conversation, I am blown away with their discussion on food groups that are good for the liver, kidneys, and eyes. They jest about medications advertised to cure headaches and other ailments. Much of what they now eat are plant-based and possibly lack nourishment, and each of them drink lots of water. *"Is this what we have to look forward to?"* I ask myself. Unfortunately, Nolan has to leave early now due to having a trumpet lesson today. Before he leaves, Nolan talks about eating cheese and other dairy foods, but Richard mentions how his sons are managing his diet. Before leaving he reminds them to have their prostates checked. Nolan runs 12 miles per day, and though it keeps him healthy, and the men applaud him, Kevin and Richard shudder at the thought. Richard reminds the group that one day they were riding the bus heading to the next gig and Nolan had to use the restroom. The bus driver let him out, but drove off,

The Fourth Movement

attempting to leave him behind, but Nolan was such a good runner that he caught up with the bus. They all laugh at remembering that event.

While reflecting, they discuss learning to swim as young, black men. Richard says he was pushed in the pool in the military because he couldn't swim, and they had to hoist him out of the pool. He was forced to take lessons shortly after. Kevin reflects on his swimming lessons and how quickly he learned, especially since he had an attractive instructor. They continue discussing hip replacements, Lasik surgery, the importance of stretching, incorporating swimming in your wellness routine, and light weightlifting. Running from bears in the woods, being sprayed by bear mace, and how not to bother those burly, protected animals are being discussed as part of their mental fodder. Kevin shares a new reflection of a runner in the woods who was taking part in a race. The runner called his mom letting her know that he felt a bear was tracking him. Surely enough, it was true. The bear caught up to him and killed him.

"People don't realize bears are faster than we think." Richard says.

As the session comes to an end, they discuss football, whose team is winning and losing, and Richard not expecting to live as long as he has.

"I'm the baby, and all of my other siblings are in their 90's." Richard says. Kevin assures him that he will live just as long. Richard says he doesn't want to be laid up, and he doesn't travel much anymore. Each of them says they just wanna enjoy life, play some gigs, and enjoy the time that remains. They're satisfied on their careers as they have been and as they are. Richard reflects on the wonder of YouTube and finding his music as well as seeing himself playing in certain bands on the channel. He wondered how it got there reminding us all that things change consistently and keeping up with the changes is both fascinating and challenging.

As they are still enjoying one another's time together, Althea enters the room and pokes her face in the screen to say hello, and to remind the men that it's time to end the "party. Richard wants to watch his football game, and Kevin has to leave as well. George left early so another Zoom party is planned at a later date. Althea, in her loving tone tells them to "end in prayer" and then close it out. Both Kevin and Richard laugh heartily, and they shout to one another, "I love you" and "good-bye" and the call ends.

Acknowledgments

OF ALL THE THINGS I'VE DONE IN MY LIFE, I am most proud of my relationship with Christ, my relationship with my wife of 44-plus years, Althea, and my sons Damion and Darius and their accomplishments and contributions to the world in which they excel. Without the velvet hammer of discipline instilled in me from my mother to work hard, and being a man of my word, and fearing the back hand of Boom Boom at any given moment because of my smart mouth, I would not be who I am today. Without their love, support, and guidance I would be lost. The friendships I have forged over the past seven decades are ones I'll cherish forever. Each of you are the notes on my sheet music, and the sound in God's ear is amazing!

I thank God I have lived as long as I have because my beginning would dictate, I should have died as an infant. I guess God had a plan for me. Being named a Living Legend, playing in various venues all over the world, was just a lifetime gig to me. I didn't realize I was making history. I just loved to play music. I have tried to stay humble, and I credit this to my upbringing, and my mother's words about not being too proud. The hit from the umbrella so long ago remains a reminder to me to stay humble.

To the younger cats who desire this same result on how to carry themselves, I say, "Don't get too proud because what goes up comes down. How you go up determines if you stay up as opposed to just dropping down. You can be as proud as you want, go high, and then come down just as fast. Don't forget the people that helped you along the way. I'll never forget the cats that helped me through all the stuff I've been through. Don't get involved in nonsense. I never did. Some of the guys I played with had drinking problems and drug problems, but I never got caught up in that. They would always say, *"Reid don't smoke, he don't drink, he don't do nothin', but play that Bass."* And my reply would be, *"that's all I'm supposed to do."* All I have ever wanted is to play my Bass, be with my family, and God has blessed me to do that. As far as I'm concerned, that's all I need.

www.ingramcontent.com/pod-product-compliance
Lightning Source LLC
Chambersburg PA
CBHW060841050426
42453CB00008B/783